QUICK START GUIDE TO LEARNING LINUX ON THE RASPBERRY PI

CARMELITO ANDRADE

Contents

Acknowledgements

Writing a book is more challenging than I thought and more rewarding than I could have imagined. I would like to express my gratitude to many people, who provided support, talked things over, read and offered valuable comments.

I owe a special thanks to my technical editor Savira Travasso, who assisted with editing and feedback. And Maclean Barretto for proofreading.

I'm eternally grateful to the Raspberry Pi community on the world wide web, for all their support and helpful blog posts, especially in the first couple of years when the first Raspberry Pi board was released in 2012-2013. And many thanks to all the active community members who unselfishly blog about their issues, reply to the forum posts and encourage beginners to learn about Linux.

And lastly, a big thanks to the Raspberry Pi foundation for putting out awesome hardware every year and consistently improving the Raspberry Pi hardware while keeping the base price the same. In addition to updating the operating system to stay in line with the latest versions of Debian GNU/Linux. And finally, for also putting out excellent documentation, books and magazines that can be downloaded for free (but we suggest you contribute if you can afford it before downloading, so that the Raspberry Pi foundation can continue their incredible work).

Who Is This Book For?

I applaud and thank you for buying this book and would like to believe that you have already taken steps to buy the latest version of the Raspberry Pi board or have a Raspberry Pi project in mind.

This book introduces you to the Raspberry Pi 4 hardware and the Raspberry Pi Operating system based on Linux. Teachers and students can learn about the various applications in Linux for everyday use and the command line tool, which is explained in an easy-to-understand format. After a couple of weeks of learning and practising the Linux command line, the student can dive into more advanced topics like shell scripting, covered in the book's last few chapters.

In addition, this book is ideal for hobbyists/Makers who want to quickly get up to speed with Linux and start using the Raspberry Pi for their next project. The book also details how to use the Raspberry Pi Camera and a USB webcam, which can come in handy if the project is related to vision sensing.

For 90% of the book, you don't need to own a Raspberry Pi to start. You can start with any Linux based operating system based on Debian, like Ubuntu, Linux Mint, etc., Or you can install the Raspberry Pi operating system on your laptop/computer and have it dual boot. This means you can enjoy both Microsoft Windows/MacOS and Raspberry Pi Operating systems on the same hardware.

The book will also come in handy as a reference at all levels of expertise, especially the last few chapters that take you through troubleshooting common issues.

CHAPTER I

What is the Raspberry Pi?

The Raspberry Pi is a small, low-cost computer that is the size of a credit card but can be as powerful as a high-value big-sized computer/laptop available today. It is plugged into a monitor just like other desktop computers and uses a mouse and a keyboard as input devices.

It enables people of all ages to explore computing at a fraction of the cost compared to a regular laptop or desktop computer and to learn how to program in languages like Scratch and Python. It's capable of doing everything you'd expect a desktop computer to do, from browsing the internet and playing high-definition video, to making spreadsheets, word-processing, and playing games.

Raspberry Pi also has the ability to interact with the outside world and has been used in a wide array of Maker projects, from building music machines, DIY gaming arcades to weather stations and tweeting birdhouses with infra-red cameras. The motive behind developing the Raspberry Pi was to encourage hands-on learning in the domain of computer science.

Who should use the Raspberry Pi?

Raspberry Pi is a device that has made it possible for people of all age groups and almost all strata of society to explore the world of computing. It can do everything a regular computer can do, from browsing the internet to word-processing and playing video games. So if you are looking for a computer to handle daily needs like watching youtube videos, listening to music or doing some word processing, the Raspberry Pi is an ideal device

The Raspberry Pi has the ability to interact with third-party software and hardware, which has drawn the eyes of everyone from individuals making standalone Wifi music systems to parents making camera-based solutions to monitor their babies. Anybody who wants to transform an engineering concept into an interactive electronics project, prototype, or work of art, should consider using the Raspberry Pi today.

If you are a teacher, the availability of the Scratch visual programming tool on the Raspberry Pi is an excellent way to engage students with both computer programming and learning the basics of electronics.

One of the benefits of Raspberry Pi is that it is not necessary to have an intimate knowledge of Linux or Python before beginning a project with Raspberry Pi. So this is ideal for young school and secondary grade students to learn the basics of Linux and programming by creating engaging projects.

The Raspberry Pi platform enables additional development and customisation to meet specific project needs for more advanced users and engineering students with electronics or computing knowledge. Again, such advanced customisation is not trivial, and you will need knowledge and skills from multiple streams like - Linux operating systems, programming and basic electronics. This book aims to provide you with enough knowledge of Linux and python programming to get a good foundation to start on some complex projects.

With new technologies like the Internet of Things (IoT) and Machine Learning emerging, the Raspberry Pi is a great hardware platform to learn about so that you can program and try out these technologies for a fraction of the cost.

Who created the Raspberry Pi ? and why?

In 2012, the Raspberry Pi Foundation launched the Raspberry Pi, a single-board computer designed to teach programming skills, build hardware projects, explore industrial applications of computer technology, etc. The goal of the Raspberry Pi Foundation is to introduce young people to hardware and software programming to facilitate their entry into programming and electronics.

The Raspberry Pi Foundation promotes the study of basic computer science in schools with a single-board computer called Raspberry Pi. One of the founders of Raspberry Pi, Eben Upton, created the first Raspberry Pi in an attempt to solve the problem of a dwindling student population in computing science at the University of Cambridge. The simplicity and ease of access led Raspberry Pi to become the UK's best-selling personal computer, selling over two million units within two years of production while encouraging everyone with interest to study and play. Sales from Raspberry Pi products fund charitable work that promotes understanding of computers and technology use in education and developing countries.

Live groups and community events are another essential part. Groups include CoderDojos for young people ages 7 to 17, school-based Code Clubs for ages 9 to 13, and Raspberry Jams (meetups for people of all ages). The events and groups are growing in popularity throughout the world, with volunteers old and young, leading participants through discovery, problem-solving, coding, and building Raspberry Pi projects. Competitions and events also take place throughout the year that stimulates learning and encourages collaboration, creativity, and real-world problem-solving.

What are some famous projects done with the Raspberry Pi?

Once you go through the first half of this book you should be comfortable with the Raspberry Pi Linux-based Operating system. And you will be in an excellent spot to try some of the notable projects mentioned below.

Make your old TV a Smart TV - using the Kodi Media player

Kodi (formerly XBMC) is a free and open-source media centre that allows you to access a full library of movies, TV shows, music, your holiday photo gallery and more. Installing Kodi on the Raspberry Pi is a breeze. It is similar to downloading the Kodi operating system image file from the Raspberry Pi downloads website and flashing it onto an SD card using software like Etcher.

Kodi Plugins give you access to a wide range of functionality like additional channels and movies. You can install equivalent plugins to watch Youtube, Netflix, Disney+, Tubi, Crackle, etc. And if you are into documentaries, you should try the National Geographic and Seeker add-ons, which have a huge catalogue of science, technology and culture shows.

Kodi isn't just for passive entertainment media. You can also play games on Kodi. Pick from a large number of emulators, or even play a stand-alone game. To control Kodi you can either use a wireless keyboard connected to the Pi or an App from the Android play store like - Yatse.

Video Game emulation using RetroPie

The most popular video game emulation library on the Pi is RetroPie. It is free, can be installed in minutes, and allows you to play thousands of your favourite vintage video games, like Street fighter II, Pacman, Tetris, etc., and even obscure ones.

RetroPie sits on top of an entire OS, and you can install it on an existing Raspberry Pi Operating system or start with the RetroPie SD image and add additional software later. It's up to you. RetroPie allows you to emulate popular video game consoles, such as the Nintendo Entertainment System, (NES), Super Nintendo (SNES), Game Boy, Nintendo 64, Sega Genesis, and more. Games are loaded as individual ROM files which can then be read by each system in RetroPie.

It's easy to find ROMs for RetroPie. There are several different types of ROMs, including copyrighted, abandonware, public domain, and homebrew games. While you can find game ROMs on any Torrent site, you shouldn't download any copyrighted titles as this may be illegal. You can also find a ton of free legal ROMs on websites, like MAME, Zophar, PDROMs, and other sites. You can also find ways to install games like Super Mario, Zelda, etc., but note these games are privacy protected.

You need a controller if you want to play retro games on RetroPie. But not all controllers are created equal, and the best one for you depends on what you want to play, how you like to play, and how much you're willing to spend. Most compatible controllers are USB only, but a few wireless controllers are supported, for example, Xbox one. But if you don't want to burn a hole in your wallet while buying a USB controller, try - Classic wired SNES Controllers with D-pad, Start, Select, A, B, X, and Y buttons.

You can also install Kodi on RetroPie for a more seamless setup.

Security Camera

Make your own DIY Raspberry Pi security camera using motionEyeOS, a customised Linux distribution for turning your Pi into a surveillance camera. The security camera can be used to record uninvited guests at your front door, monitor children in their cribs, or keep an eye on your pets.

MotionEyeOS, a free open-source application, allows you to turn a Raspberry Pi with a camera into a home video monitoring system, where the photos and videos can either stay on your device (and home network) or, if you choose, be uploaded automatically to a cloud-storage service, such as Google Drive or Dropbox. As you guessed, for this, you will need a Pi camera or a USB webcam, we will discuss this in detail in Chapter X.

Block ads using Pi-hole on the Raspberry Pi

Pi-hole has the ability to block traditional website advertisements as well as advertisements in unconventional places, such as smart TVs and mobile operating system advertisements.

While traditional ad blockers block ads after they've passed through your network, Pi-Hole essentially allows your Pi to act as a DNS (Domain Name System) server, blocking ads network scripts before using your precious network bandwidth. Because Pi-hole blocks domains at the network level, it is also called a DNS sinkhole. It can block advertisements, such as banner advertisements on a webpage, but it can also block advertisements in unconventional locations, such as, on Android, iOS and smart TVs.

Many users report seeing as much as a 25% reduction in network traffic. In other words, 25% of their former traffic was ad-related.

Turn your Pi into Amazon Echo (Alexa)

All you need to build your own Raspberry Pi Amazon Echo is a USB microphone and your Pi. You don't need to buy an Amazon echo dot, but you can set one up yourself. And this can be a fun project that's a great introduction to running third-party voice control systems on the Pi.

Alexa on Pi was created for educational purposes. You'll get a glimpse of how Alexa works behind the scenes and possibly spark an interest in designing your own custom device with Alexa embedded. Amazon has made this Pi project possible to encourage device manufacturers to embed Alexa in their products. And to this effect, you will see a lot of new smart TVs and Phones coming with Alexa support built-in.

Weather Station

Raspberry Pi can be used to build a weather station for collecting local climate and environmental data. First, you will develop and build a prototype weather station using a breadboard, jumper wires, and sensors to collect the temperature, humidity, Air Quality, Wind speed, rainfall, etc.

Once you've got everything running and tested, you can turn this prototype into a more robust build so that you can deploy it outside your home.

Just in case you want to keep it simple and are yet to learn about breadboarding an electronic circuit and soldering electronic components together. You can try using Enviro PHAT, a circuit board designed by a company called Pimoroni that plugs on top of the Pi, and has a small display to show temperature, pressure and humidity inside your home.

Home Automation using home-assistant.io

There are tons of Raspberry Pi smart home related projects which are possible, including an automatic smart watering system, security system array cameras, to a texting doorbell. Among the easiest DIY Raspberry Pi projects is a Raspberry Pi smart home hub.

Home Assistant is a top choice as an open-source intelligent Pi Raspberry home automation software option. It's available as a standalone Raspberry Pi image at home-assistant.io/installation/raspberrypi, and needs to be downloaded and flashed onto an SD card. The software is an open-source platform for controlling and automating smart home devices. It's compatible with many services such as Google Nest thermostat, Samsung SmartThings, Philips Hue, etc. Home Assistant doesn't control devices, it's simply a master hub for aggregating various smart home services into one device. Since it's on-premises, Home Assistant passes no data through cloud services. It's also incredibly intuitive and inexpensive to set up.

It can be accessed through a web-based user interface using Companion Android and iOS apps or by voice commands via a supported virtual assistant such as Google Assistant, or Amazon Alexa.

Build Your Own Raspberry Pi Cloud Server With Nextcloud

Cloud storage is an essential part of modern life. The downside is that your data is stored on remote servers by a faceless corporation which you have to trust with the privacy and security of your precious documents and photos. However, another option is hosting your files on your very own cloud server running on a computer in your home or office. One of the most popular services for achieving this is Nextcloud.

Nextcloud is a suite of client-server software for creating and using file hosting services. Nextcloud is functionally similar to Dropbox or Google Drive when used with its integrated office suite solutions. It can be hosted in the cloud or on-premises. It is scalable from home office solutions based on the low-cost Raspberry Pi all the way through to full-sized data center solutions that support millions of users.

Nextcloud has an app store with many extensions, which provides functionality like Calendars, Contact, Streaming Media, photo gallery, RSS feed reader, etc.

OctoPrint: Control and monitor your 3D Printer remotely

If you're into 3D printing and the Raspberry Pi, OctoPrint is a must-have. OctoPrint allows you to control and monitor your 3D printer remotely; no more manually dropping files onto an SD card. OctoPrint is an open-source 3D printer controller application which provides a web interface for connected printers. It displays printers' status and critical parameters and allows users to schedule prints and remotely control the printer

Simply install the OctoPrint image on your SD card for the Pi, and connect your Pi to your 3D printer's USB port. Connect an optional Raspberry Pi camera if you want to view your printer in action remotely.

The above are just a handful of applications/projects that you can do with the Pi. There are so many more projects on the internet and Raspberry Pi community, website like - building your own plant monitoring and watering system, FM radio, installing a Minecraft Game Server, digital photo frame to display family photos, etc.

If you have questions/need help where should you go?

One of the most impressive aspects of Raspberry Pi is the amount and variety of support available to users of Raspberry Pi. The Foundation website - www.raspberrypi.org contains forums, help guides, projects, blogs, videos, and troubleshooting guides. The website is an excellent resource for self-motivated individual learners, parents, and teachers and presents the information in an easy-to-grasp format. In addition to the website resources, the support for educators is extensive. From online training courses to magazines, curricula, and face-to-face academies, the Foundation has ensured that educators have the tools necessary to lead students through the fascinating discovery of computer technology.

The official documentation for the Raspberry Pi is written by the Raspberry Pi Foundation and can be found at www.raspberrypi.org/documentation/. It includes getting started, configuration guides to Linux distributions, and more.

The Raspberry Pi press also publishes a magazine called - The MagPi, which is the official Raspberry Pi magazine. It is written for the community and packed with Pi-themed projects, computing and electronics tutorials, how-to guides, and the latest community news and events. The MagPi magazine is committed to open source and operates under a Creative Commons Attribution-NonCommercial-ShareAlike 3.0. This means you are welcome to share and adapt the magazine content as long as you follow the licence terms. In addition, you can download DRM-free PDFs of every issue from the website - www.magpi.raspberrypi.com/. But as a suggestion, if you can afford it is always a good idea to get a subscription to the magazine's hard copy.

In addition to the above Raspberry Pi community is also active on various other electronic hardware community websites like community.element14.com, hackster.io/raspberry-pi , etc. And there is also a topic for raspberry-pi on stackoverflow.com, which is a go-to site for developers and engineers when they run into an issue with programming or software on their computer.

CHAPTER II

Raspberry Pi Hardware

A traditional computer has all its parts hidden inside a case known as a chassis. But the Raspberry Pi has all the components visible to the eyes. The fact that all the components are displayed in the open, makes it easy to learn about the various parts of the computer. And makes it convenient to understand what goes where when you want to plug in external peripherals like a mouse, keyboard, speaker, HDMI for display, etc. The image below shows the top view of the Raspberry Pi.

Raspberry Pi 4 Model B is the latest product in the popular Raspberry Pi range of computers, as of today while publishing this book. It offers ground-breaking increases in processor speed, multimedia performance, memory, and connectivity compared to the prior-generation Raspberry Pi 3 Model B+, while retaining backwards compatibility and similar power consumption. For the end-user, the Raspberry Pi 4 Model B provides desktop performance comparable to entry-level x86 personal computer systems.

If you purchased your Raspberry Pi as a part of the starter kit, you would have most peripherals needed to get up and running. And this is recommended if you are a beginner because all the components plug and play with each other easily.

Processor

The brain of the Raspberry Pi 4 Model B called the processor, is built around the Broadcom BCM2711, a 64-bit quad-core Arm Cortex-A72 clocked at 1.5GHz.It runs a lot faster than you'd expect, more than fast enough that it's a viable desktop replacement for your average user.

It can be found just above the centre point on the top side of the board, covered in a metal cap and called system-on-chip(SoC), which is a great indicator of what you would find if you prised the metal cover off, a silicon chip, known as an integrated circuit, which contains the bulk of Raspberry Pi's system. This includes the central processing unit (CPU), commonly thought of as the 'brain' of a computer, and the graphics processing unit (GPU), which handles the visual side of things, basically, the graphics displayed on the monitor.

Memory

A brain is no good without memory, located just to the right of the main processor, which looks like a small, black, plastic rectangle. This is Raspberry Pi's random access memory (RAM). When you're working on Raspberry Pi, the RAM holds what you're doing, only when you save your work, will it be written to the microSD card. Together, these components form Raspberry Pi's volatile and non-volatile memories. The volatile RAM loses its contents whenever Raspberry Pi is powered off, while the non-volatile microSD card keeps its contents.

Unlike any previous board, the new Raspberry Pi 4 is available in three different models, each offering different memory options. The new board can come with either 1GB, 2GB, 4GB or 8GB of RAM.

SD Card Slot

If you turn the board on its back, you will see a micro SD card slot. A micro SD card acts like a hard disk of your laptop, in the case of the Raspberry Pi, and is non-volatile memory. The Operating System (OS) installed/flashed on a micro SD card is required for booting the device.

The Operating System for all Raspberry Pi products is Linux. Linux is an open-source Operating System that interfaces between the computer's hardware and software programs. The language used with Raspberry Pi is Python – a general-purpose and high-level programming language used to develop Graphical User Interface (GUI) applications, websites, and web applications.

Power Supply

Keeping up with the latest trend, the Pi 4 has made the switch from micro USB to USB-C. For the best results, you should use the official Raspberry Pi USB Type-C Power Supply. This power supply is rated at 5V with 3 Amps current output.

Remember, this is a power supply for Raspberry Pi and not for your USB C phone, so if you plan to charge your phone with the Pi power supply, you can run the risk of damaging it.

Wireless connectivity

At the top right of the board, you'll find another metal lid covering the radio, this component gives the Raspberry Pi the ability to communicate with devices wirelessly. The radio itself acts as two main components -

- WiFi radio, for connecting to computer networks, via a WiFi router to access the internet.
- Bluetooth radio to connect to peripherals like bluetooth speaker, mouse, etc.

Wireless support is provided in an RF shielded module by the same Cypress CYW43455 chip as we saw on the Raspberry Pi 3, Model B+. Offers dual-band 2.4GHz and 5GHz IEEE 802.11.b/g/n/ac wireless networking, as well as Bluetooth 5.0 and Bluetooth LE.

Ports

The new Raspberry Pi board has Gigabit Ethernet to connect your LAN cable.

And two USB 3.0 ports which are ideal for USB 3.0 storage devices like Harddisks, as well as a couple more legacy USB 2 ports to connect a keyboard, mouse etc.

Video

The Pi 4 when compared to its older predecessor, also has a new type of video ports. Gone is the full-sized HDMI jack offered by previous generations of Raspberry Pi boards. However, in its place are two micro-HDMI ports, and that means the new Raspberry Pi 4 has dual monitor support, supporting one 4K screen at 60fps, or two 4K screens at 30fps.

Audio Jack

Alongside the two micro-HDMI ports is a 3.5 mm AV jack with 4-pole stereo output to connect to the speaker or a set of headphones.

40 pin GPIO Header

The GPIO (General-Purpose Input/Output) header is a feature of Raspberry Pi used to talk to additional hardware like LEDs and buttons to sensors like temperature humidity sensors, pulse-rate monitors etc. For this, you will have to have basic knowledge of electronics to build/ breadboard circuits.

In addition, the 40-pin GPIO header is also used to connect to HATs(Hardware Attached on Top), which are expansion circuit boards that provide extra functionality to the Pi such as motors, sensors and light without having to mess with wires to create a circuit.

Display Port

At the top edge of the board is another similar black and white connector, which appears to be identical to the camera connector. But this is the exact opposite and is a display connector, or Display Serial Interface (DSI), designed for use with a Raspberry Pi Touch Display. The Raspberry Pi 7 inch touch requires two connections to the Pi, that is power from the Pi's GPIO port and a ribbon cable that connects to the DSI port. Touchscreen has drivers which support 10-finger touch and an on-screen keyboard.

PoE HAT Header

Just below and to the left of this header is another smaller header with four pins, this is used to connect the Power over Ethernet (PoE) HAT, an optional add-on which lets Raspberry Pi receive power from a network connection rather than the USB Type-C port.

Peripherals

The Raspberry Pi 4 cannot do a lot by itself, just like a regular computer cannot function independently. The Raspberry Pi Foundation has the following set of official accessories

- Raspberry Pi Case to keep board safe from dust and impact
- USB Keyboard
- USB Mouse

- Camera Module which we will learn about in detail in Chapter VIII
- 7 inch Touch display connects to DSI, just in case you want to make your Pi portable instead of connecting it to a monitor every time.
- SenseHAT was created with a sensor to measure temperature, humidity, accelerations, pressure, 3D orientation and a 8x8 LED matrix. And this was sent to the International Space Station to run experiments created by school children.

If someone were to quiz you on the exacts of the Raspberry Pi 4 model B, here are the details

Processor: Broadcom BCM2711, quad-core Cortex-A72 (ARM v8) 64-bit SoC @ 1.5GHz

Memory: 1GB, 2GB, 4GB or 8GB LPDDR4 (depending on model) with on-die ECC

Connectivity: 2.4 GHz and 5.0 GHz IEEE 802.11b/g/n/ac wireless
LAN, Bluetooth 5.0, BLE
Gigabit Ethernet
2 × USB 3.0 ports
2 × USB 2.0 ports.

GPIO: Standard 40-pin GPIO header (fully backwards-compatible with previous boards)

Video & sound: 2 × micro HDMI ports (up to 4Kp60 supported)
2-lane MIPI DSI display port
2-lane MIPI CSI camera port
4-pole stereo audio and composite video port

SD card support: Micro SD card slot for loading operating system and data storage

Input power: 5V DC via USB-C connector (minimum 3 Amps)

What are the other versions of the Raspberry Pi?

The Raspberry Pi grew more and more powerful as the years went by, with increasing processing power and adding connectivity like WiFi and Bluetooth. Here is a little history of the progression and the various single-board computers released by the Raspberry Pi foundation.

Original Raspberry Pi Model A/B

The very first model of Raspberry Pi was known as the Model B, followed by the Model A, released in 2012 and 2013 respectively. Both models had the Broadcom BCM 2835 SoC within them, but had different specifications:

Model B had either 256 MB or 512 MB of RAM depending on the date of the purchase, a 10/100 wired network/ethernet port, and two USB ports.

Model A, for instance, had 256 MB of RAM, one USB port, and zero networking qualities.

These models were distinguishable because of their smaller than usual GPIO port, which has only 26 pins. Both models also possess a full-size SD card storage which you normally use with your DSLR cameras, instead of the compact microSD cards that the newer models come with.

Raspberry Model A+/B+

The original models proved to be very popular, but more than swiftly replaced with a new board design called the Plus which was released in 2014. These later model iterations came with the 40-pin GPIO header while improving some of the other features. However, they didn't deviate from the BCM 2835 SoC, which means that there was not much of a difference in performance between the Plus models and the older models.

The hardware difference between the Model A+ and Model B+ is similar to the previous Model A and Model B. The A+ model, which has a smaller footprint than the A Model, either has a 256 or 512 MB of memory depending on the launch of the product, zero network capabilities, and a single USB port; the Model B+ has 512 MB of memory, a 10/100 wired network port, and four USB ports.

Raspberry Pi 2

Where the plus and previous other boards use the same BCM 2835 SoC processor, the newer Raspberry Pi 2 uses the new BCM 2836 SoC processor and was released in 2015. Instead of one core like the original, the new processor features over four cores as well as 4 to 8 times the performance of the original - which makes everything from word processing to compiling code a much faster process. This new version also contains over 1GB (1024 MB) of RAM, doubling what was available for the previous version, which made memory intensive applications and multitasking go much smoother and a lot more responsive.

When it comes to layout, not much has changed from Model B+. For instance, the Raspberry Pi 2 has the same four USB ports, 40-pin GPIO header, 10/100 wired network ports as well as other ports. If you indeed have an add-on device or a case that works with the Model B+, it will work well with the Raspberry Pi 2, but potentially faster.

The new board comes with bigger software compatibility than the previous versions, in addition to the Raspbian operating system, a proprietary operating system like Windows 10 IoT Core and Ubuntu were made available, which wasn't made available for the Raspberry Pi's predecessors.

Raspberry Pi Zero

The Raspberry Pi Zero is by far not only the smallest board in the entire Raspberry Pi family, but it's also the cheapest of them all and was released in 2015. Despite being the size of a couple of sticks of chewing gum that are stacked on top of each other, the Raspberry Pi Zero hardly lacks what the other models have, it has the same BCM 2835 SoC as well as 512 MB of RAM like the Raspberry Pi Model B+, and runs at a slightly faster speed for better performance.

However, Pi Zero being smaller in size has certain caveats. The mini-HDMI port and single micro-USB port require adapters before they can be connected to standard peripherals, like a monitor, USB keyboard and Mouse. There is no DSI port, the 3.5 mm AV jack is gone, the CSI port needs a different type of ribbon cable to connect the camera, and while it's present, the GPIO header needs pins that have to be purchased separately and soldered into place before it can be used.

If you're a beginner the Pi Zero is not for you. But if you are a more experienced user and want to bring more intelligence to embedded projects especially to keep the cost low, while keeping the power draw, and size small - the Pi Zero is the board you need to get familiar with.

Raspberry Pi 3 Model B

The last model before the fourth iteration, the Raspberry Pi 3, came with a newer processor at the time: the Broadcom BCM 2837. Being the 64-bit processor, not 32-bit, the new processor was considerably faster than the BCM 2836 found in the Raspberry Pi 2 version, which at the time was a massive upgrade from the BCM 2835 of the original and the Plus series. The Raspberry Pi 3 was also the first model to get built-in wireless support, which included a radio that connected to 2.4 GHz Wi-Fi networks and Bluetooth devices.

Like Pi 2, nothing much was changed with the layout: you would get the same four USB ports, 40-pin GPIO header, 10/100 wired network port, and several other ports that came with the last models.

One great advantage of the new Pi 3, other than the built-in wireless features and, the improved performance, is its 64-bit processor. Switching over to this model given its new processor means that you will have better software compatibility performance and security over the 32-bit version of the previous models.

Raspberry Pi Zero W

The Raspberry Pi Zero W was released in 2017 and sought to introduce the same connectivity improvements the Pi 3 Model B included without sacrificing the board's tiny size.

This version of the Raspberry Pi tried to retain the tiny size of the original Pi Zero while adding support for Bluetooth (4.1 BLE) and Wi-Fi (b/g/n single-band 2.4GHz) onto the board. Besides including this new connectivity module, the Raspberry Pi introduced no other significant changes with the Pi Zero W. All other functionality remains the same as the original board. Even the power requirements remained the same.

Raspberry Pi 3 Model B+ and A+

The Raspberry Pi 3 Model B+ was released in 2018 and introduced numerous improvements across several areas. While this version of the Raspberry Pi was only marketed as a "plus" model, it brought a wealth of changes that made it well worth upgrading from the original Pi 3 Model B.

The first changes were made to the Pi's processor, boosting the clocks speed even higher than the standard Pi 3. This would also be the first Raspberry Pi to see a boost made to the GPU clock speeds. With this release, the processor's clock speed was increased from 1.2GHz to 1.4 GHz. Additionally, the GPU saw a clock boost from 250MHz to 400 MHz.

This release saw the Pi finally get a full gigabit Ethernet port. Previous versions of the Raspberry Pi were limited to 100 Mbit/s. Now you can theoretically handle up to 1000 Mbit/s using a Pi 3 Model B+.

In addition to these changes, the Pi foundation also made improvements to the Wi-Fi capability. The Wi-Fi supports b/g/n/ac and is dual-band capable. The new chip means you can now connect to both 2.4 GHz and 5 GHz networks and get improved speeds.

Raspberry Pi 3 Model A+ features the same size board as the original Raspberry Pi Model A+ but brings all of the performance enhancements of the Pi 3B+.

This board even has the same quad-core ARM processor clocked at 1.4 GHz introduced with the Pi 3 Model B+. The only change on the performance side was that they scaled back the amount of memory from 1

GB to 512 MB.

The Raspberry Pi 4 Model B is the latest single-board computer released in 2019 by the Raspberry Pi Foundation which is discussed in detail above.

Raspberry Pi 400

The Raspberry Pi 400 was launched in 2020 and introduced a brand new form factor to the family of Pi devices. This form factor involved the Pi coming built-in to a fully functional keyboard. This brought a new level of ease of use as you no longer needed to attach a keyboard to use the Pi.

The Raspberry Pi 400 contains the same general specifications as the Raspberry Pi 4 but is tweaked for this new form factor. Thanks to the work on the device's thermal performance, the processor on Pi 400 has an increased clock speed over the base Pi 4. As a result, the Pi 400 has an increased clock rate from 1.5 GHz to 1.8 GHz. Meaning you should get slightly better performance when using this device.

Unlike the Pi 4, there is only one variant of the Raspberry Pi 400. You can only get 4GB of memory with this device. Another change with this device is that it only has three USB ports. One is a USB 2.0 port, and the other two are USB 3.0 ports.

The rest of the specifications of the device remain the same as the Raspberry Pi 4. You have access to the same GPIO pins, gigabit ethernet, Wi-Fi, and Bluetooth as the base device.

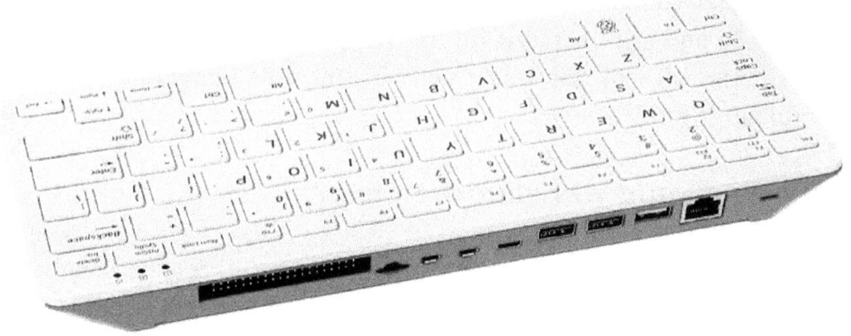

Raspberry Pi Compute modules

If you plan on including the functionality of Pi in a commercial product, for example, you want to build your own smart TV to sell to customers on eCommerce websites and stores, you will have to use the Raspberry Pi Compute module. With almost every version of the Raspberry Pi released above, a compute module was also released.

The latest version of the Raspberry Pi Compute Module 4 harnesses the compute power of the popular Raspberry Pi 4 Model B, bringing it to a smaller form factor suitable for integration into products. Key features include a high-performance 64-bit quad-core processor, dual-display support at resolutions up to 4K for video, hardware video decode at up to 4Kp60, up to 8GB of RAM, Gigabit Ethernet, USB 2.0, dual camera interfaces, and PCIe Gen 2 x1 interface.

The optional dual-band 2.4/5.0GHz wireless LAN and Bluetooth 5.0 have modular

compliance certification. This allows the board to be designed into end products with significantly reduced compliance testing, improving both cost and time to market. Either the onboard antenna or an external antenna kit can be used.

Compute Module 4 has optional onboard eMMC of 8GB, 16GB or 32GB, for the operating system and your programs.

There is one thing common between all the Raspberry Pi models, and that is backward compatibility. This means software written for any Raspberry Pi model is compatible with all other models. The compatibility is so good that you can take the OS developed for the latest model of the Raspberry Pi and still install it on the earliest model B launched in 2012. Obviously, the OS will run, but it will be a bit slow compared to the more powerful latest model.

Which Pi should you choose to buy?

If you want to follow along with this book, you should get the Raspberry Pi 4 with 4GB RAM or the Raspberry Pi 400. Also, if you're a beginner please buy the kit, which should come with the matching USB power supply, an SD card and a micro HDMI cable to connect to a monitor.

But if you know your way around Linux you can get the Raspberry Pi Zero W to follow along. Though the Pi Zero W is cheaper and has less RAM, you will have to try and use the Pi Zero W in headless mode, which means with no monitor connected. This is discussed in detail in Chapter VII.

Also, say you have ordered your Raspberry Pi and it's going to take 7 days to get to your address, or your seller/e-commerce site has the Pi on backorder, you can still get started with learning about the Raspberry Pi operating system and the range of applications, and python programming, by installing the Raspberry Pi for Desktop image on your PC(Personal Computer).

CHAPTER III

Installing & Getting Started with Raspberry Pi 4

As the Raspberry Pi is one of the favourite development boards of developers and DIYers, this chapter details step-by-step how to install the operating system and set up network connectivity to access the internet.

What do you need to get started?

Raspberry Pi

Well, if it wasn't obvious already reading the Chapters above, first, you'll need a Raspberry Pi. If you have no budget constraint you can get the Raspberry Pi 4 B 8GB model or at least the 4GB RAM model. However, you can also get the 2GB variant at a lesser price but, don't expect it to run smoothly while multitasking with multiple applications open.

USB Type-C Power Supply

Now, before you plug in your phone's USB charger which could be potentially a 5V 1.5 Amps, the Raspberry Pi 4 needs 3 Amps of current, so, make sure you use the original Raspberry Pi 4 compatible power supply, which is rated at 5V, 3 Amps.

A USB Mouse And Keyboard

To navigate in the OS, you'll be needing a USB mouse and keyboard. You can use any standard wired or wireless keyboard and mouse with the Pi.

MicroSD Card

Most newer Pi models use microSD cards for storage. Not all SD cards work perfectly, so your best bet is to either buy the official Raspberry Pi microSD card, which comes with an operating system preloaded or SanDisk 32GB Ultra microSD. You'll also need a way to plug the SD card into your computer, like a USB adapter, if your computer/laptop does not have an sd card holder slot.

HDMI cable

Pi 4 has two micro HDMI ports, allowing you to connect two separate monitors. You need either a micro HDMI to HDMI cable or a standard HDMI to HDMI cable plus a micro HDMI to HDMI adapter, to connect Raspberry Pi 4 to a Monitor.

Ethernet Cable/ WiFi Connectivity

If you intend to browse via ethernet, you can use any standard ethernet cable to connect to the internet via your network switch or router.

Case

Technically, this is optional but it is recommended. Instead of having your bare board out in the open, it's probably a good idea to protect it with a case. You can use the official Raspberry Pi 4 case which is made of red and white plastic material, or you can use a transparent Acrylic case if you want to use the Pi in a classroom setting, with all the components of the Pi visible. In addition, if you browse eCommerce sites, there are other cool cases out there, like retro gaming cases and multi-colour cases. Many cases also come with separate heatsinks and/or fans, which can aid in keeping that system-on-a-chip running cool.

As a suggestion, if you are buying a case from an ecommerce website, buy one which comes with heat sinks and a fan that you can power from the GPIO pins.

Also, as a reminder, if you are a beginner, try and get a kit, which will give you all the components above with the Raspberry Pi 4, so that every thing easily plugs and plays with each other.

Setting up operating system

The Raspberry Pi boots from a Micro SD card. The card holds the Pi's operating system and files the way a hard drive would in a PC. Many operating systems are available for the Pi and most are distributions of Linux. The operating system maintained and officially supported by the Raspberry Pi Foundation is Raspberry Pi Operating System, previously called Raspbian, which is based on Debian, optimized for the Raspberry Pi, and includes lots of useful software.

Advanced users will be familiar with installing an image to an SD card, but for beginners, an operating system installer called Raspberry Pi Imager was created to make the process easier.

The easiest way to get started is to buy a Micro SD card pre-installed. You can often buy a Raspberry Pi with the SD card included as part of the kit or you can buy the pre-installed SD card alone. But, if you have a Micro SD card lying around and would like to use that, you can easily download and install Raspberry Pi Operating System yourself, using one of these methods -

Using Raspberry Pi Imager

Raspberry Pi Imager is the quick and easy way to install Raspberry Pi OS and other operating systems to a microSD card, ready to use with your Raspberry Pi.

Download and install Raspberry Pi Imager to a computer/laptop with an SD card reader. Put the micro SD card you'll use with your Raspberry Pi into the reader and run Raspberry Pi Imager.

This is a self explanatory tool, and there are installs available for macOS, Microsoft Windows and Linux.

Using Etcher Options

Since many projects mentioned in Chapter I, will require you to flash an image to the SD card yourself, it's a good idea to learn how to do that now. Once you know how to do it, it can be simpler than NOOBS. For writing to the SD card, we recommend Etcher since it's available for Windows, macOS, and Linux.

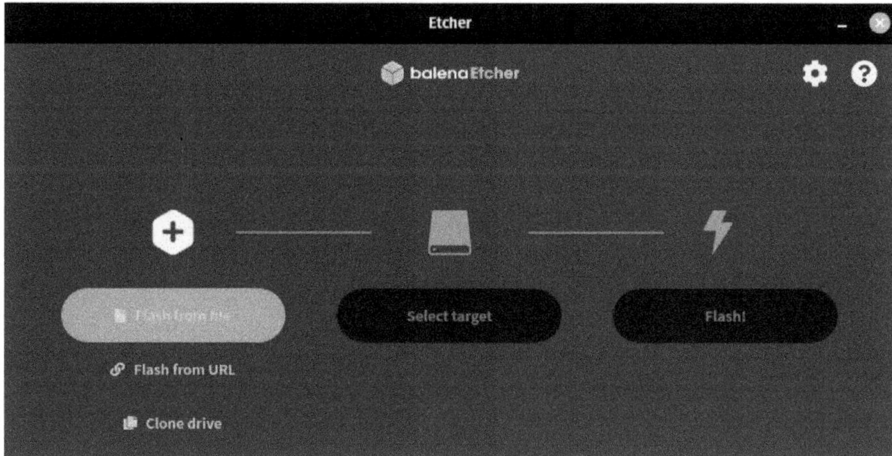

Launch Etcher, choose the raspios-xxxxx.img.xz file you just downloaded, unzip the file, choose your SD card drive, and hit Flash!. This will take a few minutes.

Connecting Everything Together

- Plug the preloaded SD Card into the SD card slot at the back of the Pi.
- Plug the USB keyboard and mouse into the Pi.
- Connect the micro HDMI cable to the micro HDMI port closest to the USB-C power input on the Pi, and then to a HDMI enabled TV or

monitor.

- Plug the power supply into the main socket.
- With your TV or monitor screen on, plug the power supply into the Pi USB C socket.
- The RPi should boot up and display the desktop on the screen in a few seconds.

It is always recommended to connect the USB C power supply to the Pi last. While most connections can be made live, it is best practice to connect items such as displays with the power turned off. The Pi may take a little longer to boot when powered-on for the first time, so be patient!

If you want a dual monitor setup for multitasking, you will need another TV or monitor, and another micro HDMI cable to connect to the second micro HDMI port on the Pi. Also, you can connect an external hard disk, and a printer to the remaining USB ports, to make the Pi a fully functional desktop machine.

CHAPTER IV

Introduction to the PIXEL Desktop

PIXEL (Pi Improved Xwindows Environment, Lightweight) is an extensively modified version of the LXDE X11 desktop environment. It was initially released in September 2016 for use with Raspberry Pi single-board computers, but now it has also been packaged up for x86 computers and laptops. This means if you are eager to get started with most of the chapters below in the book without buying the Raspberry Pi, you can install and boot your Windows or Mac PC into the PIXEL desktop environment.

PIXEL desktop is clean and modern-looking, with a wide range of productivity software and programming tools pre-installed. The Raspberry Pi has a complete operating system based on Debian GNU/Linux distribution. We will use the PIXEL desktop to carry out hands-on in the book.

GNU / Linux is the usual Operating System (OS) name that the Raspberry Pi carries. Raspberry Pi Operating system (previously called Raspbian) and Debian are nothing more than distributions of this OS. That is, Raspberry Pi OS is a selection of GNU / Linux packages compiled for a specific architecture and packaged with the help of specific tools to achieve a pleasant user experience. Instead of going here and there in search of installers and drivers as we do in Microsoft Windows, GNU specialises in packages for specific purposes. GNU means GNU's Not Unix, it is a recursive acronym. It refers to the fact that it does not contain a single line of Unix, the proprietary OS of AT&T, which is one of the largest telecommunications companies in the USA, which was then licensed to multiple international brands. The Linux suffix refers to the kernel of the operating system.

Using the desktop

When you first log in to the Pi, you are greeted with a desktop environment which is similar to your windows desktop or Mac PC. The desktop will be accompanied by a wallpaper in the background with some of the base programs that you will be using which appear on the top bar of that wallpaper. You will find a taskbar at the top of your desktop that enables you to load any program you wish to open.

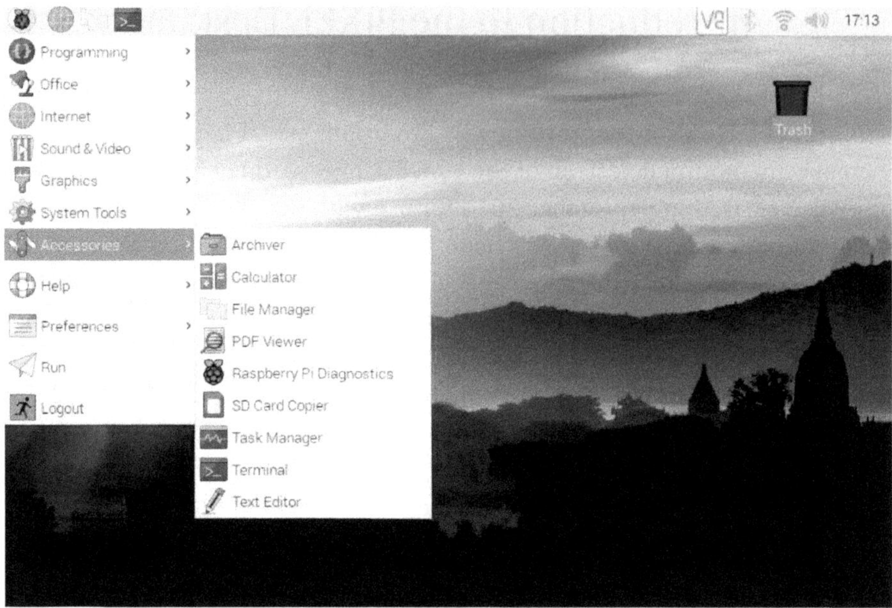

The right side of the menu bar is where you will find the system tray. If there are any removable storage devices connected to the Raspberry Pi, like USB memory sticks, then you need to click on the eject symbol to eject and remove them safely. To the far right, you'll find the timer/clock where you can bring up a digital calendar when you click on it.

Next to the timer is the speaker icon, click on the icon using the left mouse button to adjust the audio volume of your system, or you can click the right mouse button to choose the output you want your system to use. Right next to that is the network icon, you'll know that you're connected to a wireless network when you see your network signal strength is displayed in a series of bars, but if you're connected to a wired network, only two arrows will be displayed. You can bring up a list of nearby networks by clicking on the network icon, whereas the Bluetooth icon right next to it will enable you to connect to any Bluetooth device nearby.

To the left of the menu bar, you will find the Launcher, where all the programs installed on the Pi operating system can be run. Some of the programs like the browser, file manager and terminal will appear as shortcut icons, whereas others that are hidden away somewhere in the menu can be brought up by clicking the raspberry icon located on the far-left side.

Every program in the menu is split into categories and is explicitly named based on its purpose. For example, the programming category has software that allows us to write programs, which we will elaborate in the chapters below when we go through python programming. The Games category enables you to play whatever games are listed.

Desktop pictures/wallpaper

Once the desktop appears, the first thing you'll notice is the rather stunning background image. There are 18 images to choose from, you can find them using the File Manager described next at /usr/share/pixel-wallpaper/. To change the desktop wall paper, similar to Microsoft Windows Operating system you can right click and select Desktop Preference and you can use the Picture folder to choose the wall paper you prefer.

File Manager

Any file that you save - be it the programs that you write, videos you create, or the images that you download from online/from the internet - will go right to your home directory. To view your home directory, click the Raspberry icon once more to pull up the menu, point the mouse over to Accessories, and then click File Manager to load it.

With the file manager, you can browse a variety of folders, also called directories and files that are already there in the Raspberry Pi's microSD card or on any removable storage device such as a USB flash drive that you can connect to the board's USB ports. When you open it for the first time, your home directory opens up automatically. Here, you'll find lines of folders, also called subdirectories. You can click on each folder to look inside the folder or use the up and down arrow keys to traverse through the folders.

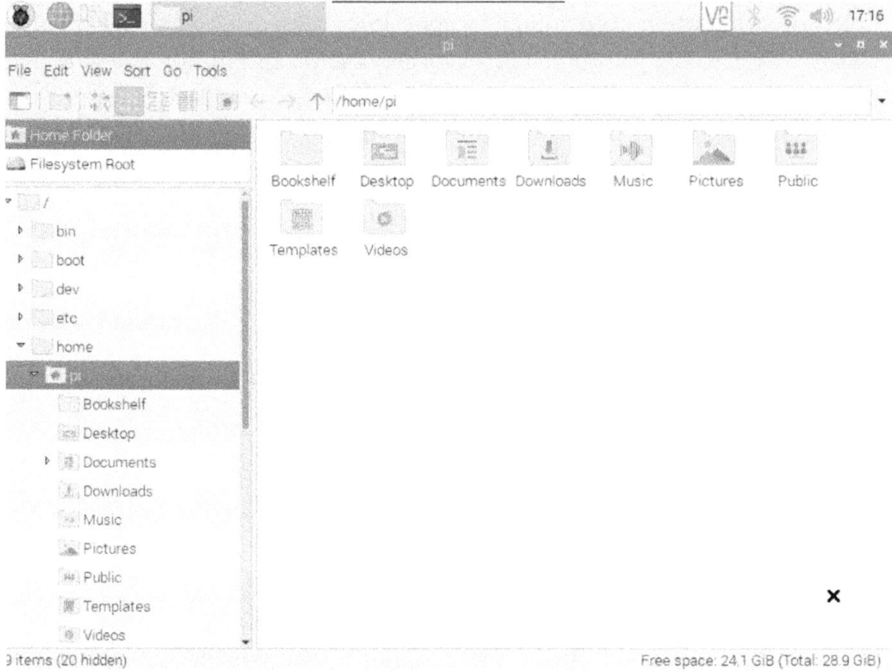

Let's first get acquainted with the structure of folders and files of the system.The text box at the top indicates /home/pi, which is the current folder. The routes of the files and folders use the character / as a separator. Remember, it is not possible to have a folder with that character in the name because the system could not differentiate it from a route of two components.

The folder / without anything in front of it is the root folder. All the other folders branch out of the root folder. The route /home/pi refers to the Pi user's home folder. The name 'home' refers to the folder containing all the personal folders like Desktop, Documents, Music, Downloads, etc. In the book, we will use the Pi user exclusively and will store all the files we create in one of the sub-folders under the Pi folder.

Navigate File Manager

There is an icon bar having useful shortcuts under the file manager's menu bar. You can use these to navigate the file manager and understand the icons that come under it.

Add Tab - Consider a scenario if you want to work in two folders at the same time. For example, copy files from one folder to another. Then, you need to quickly switch between those two folders. It enables you to have two different folders open at the same time so that you can simply click them to switch between them. You can close the tab by clicking the cross (X) icon on the tab.

Previous folder - The previous folder button, as the name implies, takes you back to the last folder, which we have accessed on that tab. It works a bit like a web browser's back button.

Next folder - Next folder button, as the name implies, takes us to a folder that we have visited after the folder on which we have been working. We will end up where we started if we first click the previous folder button and then the Next folder button.

Folder History - The Folder history button, as the name implies, will open a menu having the folders we have visited.

Up a level - There can be parent and child folders in your Raspberry Pi desktop. For example, the Desktop folder is inside the Pi folder. Hence, the Pi folder will be the parent folder, and the Desktop folder will be the child folder. The up a level button will take you to the parent folder.

Home - The home button, as the name implies, takes us back to the Pi folder.

Path - Path, as you have seen in the web browser's URL bar, is the text description of the location of the folder we are working with. It also includes the list of the folders which are above it.

Cut, copy, move files and folders

The file manager in the PIXEL desktop environment makes it easy to move your files and folders from one place to another. It also makes it easy to cut, copy, and paste your files and folders. You just need to right-click a file or folder of your choice, and a menu will appear. This menu has the following options:

- Renaming the file.
- Moving the file to the wastebasket, which is deleting the file
- Cut or copy the files.

If you want to cut the file or folder, right-click on that and choose the option Cut. After that, right-click an empty space where you want to paste that folder. From the menu that appears, select paste and your file or folder will be pasted at that empty space.

Likewise, if you want to copy the file or folder, you need to choose the option copy from the right-click menu and then, paste it wherever you want. It will create a duplicate file or folder.

Similar to the windows operating system you can also use the following keyboard shortcuts -

- Ctrl+A: To select all the files and folders.
- Ctrl+C: To copy the files and folders.
- Ctrl+V: To paste the files and folders.
- Ctrl+X: To cut the files and folders.

Sorting the files

You can sort your files in Raspberry Pi by name, size, file type, modification time, etc. For this, you again need to right-click the empty space in the right pane of the File Manager. A menu will appear, and you need to select the option to change how the files are sorted.

You can also change how your files are displayed in the File Manager. For this, you need to use the View menu on the Menu bar at the top of the File Manager. The View menu will give us the following four ways to display our files and folders:

Icon view - It is the default option used by the File Manager. It strikes a good balance between the size of each icon and the number of files we can see at one time.

Thumbnail view - Another view option is Thumbnail View, which is mostly used in a folder of images. It enlarges the preview.

Compact view - As the name implies, the Compact View lists the files and folders in columns, and this is done with a small icon and filename. It helps us to view as many files as possible at a time.

Detailed view - As the name implies, this view reveals detailed information like a short description, size, last modification date, etc., about the file.

Delete files and folders

If you want to delete a single file or folder, you can right-click that in the File Manager. From the menu, you need to choose the option Move to Trash. You can also use the keyboard Delete button to send the selected files to the wastebasket.

Sub folders under the root /

If you click on /, which is the root folder, you will see sub folder, which will not make sense if this is your first time using a Linux OS. Here is the description for some of the important folders.
/ - Primary hierarchy root and root directory of the entire file system hierarchy.

/bin - Essential command binaries that need to be available in single-user mode, including to bring up the system or repair it for all users

/boot - Boot loader files - these are responsible for booting the Pi (example - kernels, initrd)

/dev - Device files which are interface to a device driver that appears in a file system as if it were an ordinary file(example - /dev/null, /dev/disk0, /dev/sda1, /dev/tty, /dev/random).

/etc - Host-specific system-wide configuration files. These are files used to configure the parameters and initial settings for some computer programs. (example -. Your WiFi configuration file, which contains WiFi router name and user details can be found at - /etc/wpa_supplicant)

/home - Users' home directories, containing saved files, personal settings, etc.(example for the Pi user the home directory will contain a subfolder pi)

/lib - Libraries essential for the binaries in /bin and /sbin. These may include configuration data, documentation, help data, message templates, pre-written code and subroutines, classes, values or type specifications.

/media - Mount points for removable media such as CD-ROMs and USB drives.

/mnt - Temporarily mounted filesystems. Mounting is the process by which you make a filesystem available to the system. After mounting, your files will be accessible under the mount-point ./mnt. This directory usually contains mount points or sub-directories where you mount your external USB data stick or hard disk.

/opt - is reserved for the installation of add-on application software packages that are not part of the default installation.

/root - Home directory for the root user.

/sys - Contains information about devices, drivers, and some kernel features.

/usr - Secondary hierarchy for read-only user data, contains the majority of multi-user utilities and applications. It should be shareable and read-only.

/var - contains variable files, files whose content is expected to continually change during normal operation of the system, such as logs, spool files, and temporary e-mail files.

Warning: Since most of these are system folders, do not try to copy/paste or delete files in these folders.

Raspberry Pi Configuration

Click the Raspberry icon and then go to the Preferences menu, and then select Raspberry Pi Configuration. This tool is divided into four tabs, each controlling a certain part of Raspbian. By default, the configuration tool opens to its **system tab**, which has the following options -

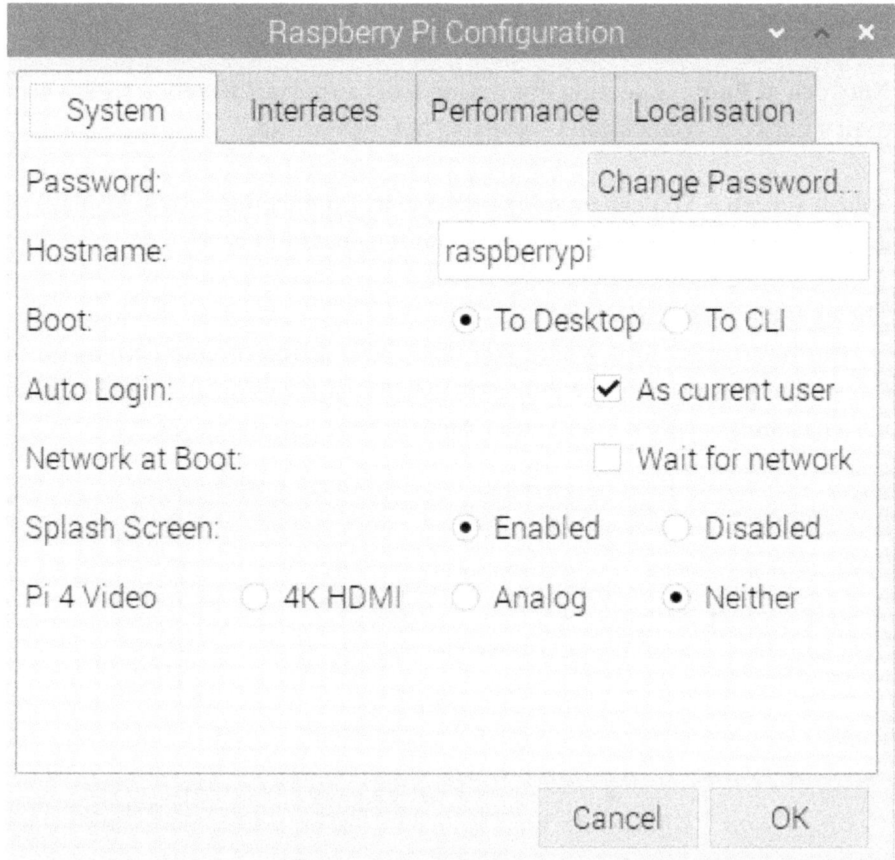

Change Password – The default password is raspberry. You can change it by clicking the change password button. This is something you should do if you plan on accessing the internet on your Pi.

Change the hostname – The default name is raspberry pi. You can also change it to the name which you want to use on the network.

Boot – You can choose from the two options and control whether Raspberry Pi boots into the desktop or CLI i.e., command line interface.

Auto Login – With the help of this option, you can set whether the user should automatically log in or you want the user to enter the password before login.

Network at Boot – selecting this option will cause your Raspberry Pi to wait until a network connection is available before starting.

Splash screen – You can enable or disable it. On enabling, it will display the graphical splash screen that shows when Raspberry Pi is booting.

The next tab is the **Interfaces**

The Interfaces tab is where you turn these different connections on or off, so that your Raspberry Pi recognises that you've linked something to it via a particular type of connection. Here are the list of options

Raspberry Pi Configuration

System | Interfaces | Performance | Localisation

Camera:	Enabled	• Disabled
SSH:	Enabled	• Disabled
VNC:	• Enabled	Disabled
SPI:	Enabled	• Disabled
I2C:	Enabled	• Disabled
Serial Port:	Enabled	• Disabled
Serial Console:	• Enabled	Disabled
1-Wire:	Enabled	• Disabled
Remote GPIO:	Enabled	• Disabled

Cancel | OK

Camera - enables the Raspberry Pi Camera Module

SSH - allows remote access to your Raspberry Pi from another computer using SSH

VNC - allows remote access to the Raspberry Pi Desktop from another computer using VNC client.

SPI - enables the SPI bus GPIO pins

I2C - enables the I2C bus GPIO pins

Serial - enables the Serial (Rx, Tx) GPIO pins

1-Wire - enables the 1-Wire GPIO pin

Remote GPIO — allows access to your Raspberry Pi's GPIO pins from another computer

Next tab is **Performance**

This is for that special project where you need to increase the performance of the Pi. But remember, changing your Raspberry Pi's performance settings may result in it behaving erratically or not working. So if you are a beginner, do not change these settings.

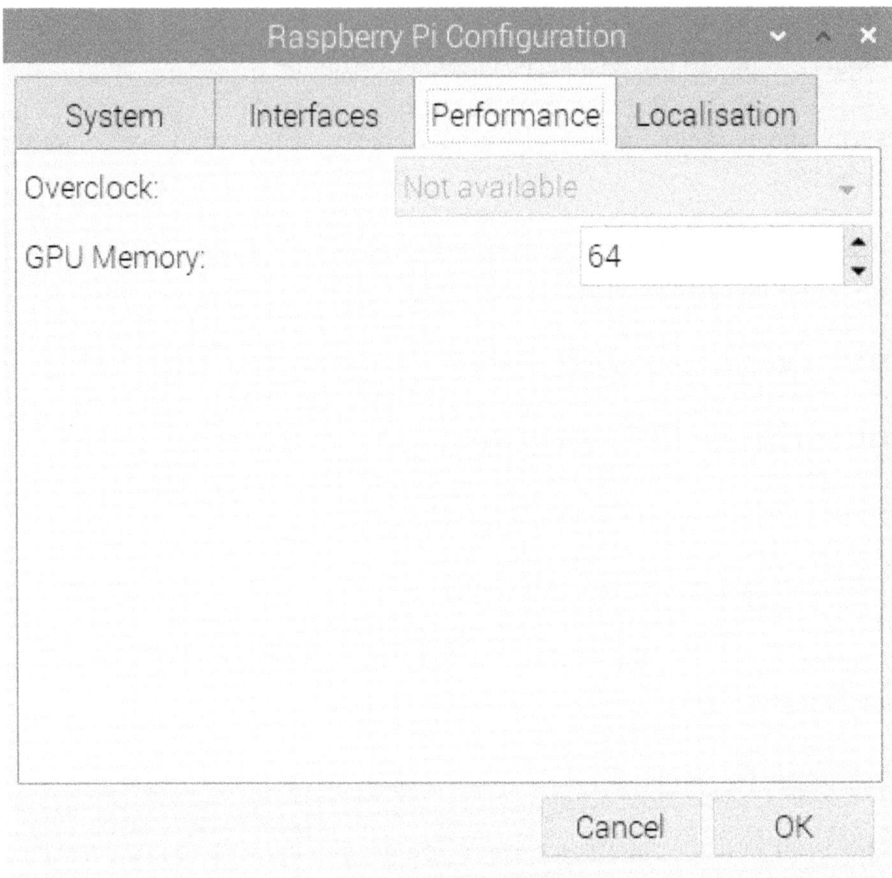

Overclock - change the CPU speed and voltage to increase performance

GPU Memory - change the allocation of memory given to the GPU

The last tab is **Localisation**

This tab allows you to change your Raspberry Pi settings to be specific to a country or location.

Locale - set the language, country, and character set used by your Raspberry Pi

Timezone - set the time zone.

Keyboard - change your keyboard layout based on the keyboard you connect.

WiFi Country - set the WiFi country code to the country you are in. Different countries have different rules about the kind of frequencies that WiFi radio can use. For instance, if you set the Wi-Fi country in the

Raspberry Pi Configuration Tool to a country other than the one you're in right now, it will confuse your device and have a struggle when connecting to your networks. What's worse is that it can also be illegal under radio licensing laws. So, in other words, don't do it.

Connecting to WiFi

At the top right, there would be icons for Bluetooth and Wi-Fi. To configure your Wi-Fi, you need to click on that icon. Once clicked, it will open a menu showing the available networks. It also shows the option to turn off your Wi-Fi. Among those available networks, you need to select a network. After selecting, it will prompt you to enter the Wi-Fi password.

If you see a red cross on the icon, it means your connection has failed or dropped.To test whether your Wi-Fi works correctly, open a Chromium web browser and visit your favourite web page.

Chromium

The first thing to do when you start using your Raspberry Pi board is to open the Chromium web browser. Before doing this, a suggestion is to change your Pi password using the Raspberry Pi configuration tool described a couple of pages ago. To open Chromium, click the blue globe button on the taskbar, or go to the internet section in the Application Menu and select Chromium.

Chromium is not hard to get used to, and those who have used Google's Chrome browser on other computers will find that it is quite similar in operation. Like any other web browser, Chromium allows you to open and view websites, communicate with several people around the world using social media platforms, chat sites, and forms, as well as play games and watch videos.

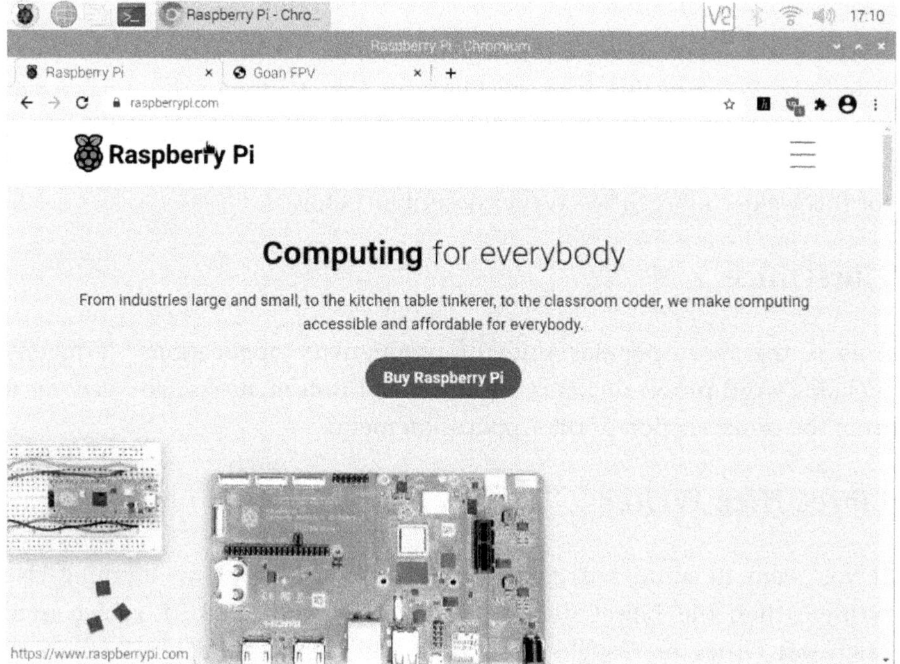

For a better experience, maximise the window of your Chromium web browser on the top right side of the Chromium window title bar, you'll find three icons. You will need to click the middle, up-arrow icon, which will maximise the window to fill the entire screen. The button to the left of the Maximize is Minimised on the taskbar, which will hide the window when you click on it. And to the right of maximising is the close function button which, of course, closes the window.

The big white bar with a magnifying glass that sits at the top left-hand side of the Chromium window is the address bar. Click in the address bar, type www.raspberrypi.org or your favourite website, and then hit ENTER on your keyboard.

To open up a new tab, you can click the Tab button that is to the extreme right side of one tab, or you can also hold the CTRL key down on your keyboard and then press the T key before you let go of CTRL. If you want to close the browser, all you have to do is hit the Close button at the top-right corner of the window.

Text Editor

PIXEL has a simple text editor, which is similar to Notepad on Microsoft Windows. You can find it by clicking the Text Editor in the Accessories menu of the Application menu. Text editor is good for writing quick notes and basic word processing but not ideal for creating print-ready documents, for this we use LibreOffice Writer described below.

LibreOffice

This is the most popular suite of productivity applications. It mainly includes word processing, spreadsheets, and presentations. You can get it from the office section of the Application menu.

LibreOffice Writer

If you want to write a document, an article, an essay, or anything else written, then the LibreOffice Writer is what you need. If you've used Microsoft Office or Google Docs, then you have a good idea of how to use LibreOffice's word processor. Besides being able to write documents, this word processor also allows you to format them in a variety of creative ways. You can change the font colour and size, insert images, tables, charts, add effects, and any other type of content you choose. Like other word processor programs, the LibreOffice Writer will inspect whatever you've written for mistakes, as well as highlight spelling and grammatical errors in red and green, respectively, as you type.

There are several icons at the top of the window that you can experiment with to see what they do: see if you can increase the font size, as well as change the colour. If you're uncertain how to get this done, move your mouse cursor over each icon one at a time to see a 'tooltip' that lets you know what the icon is about and what it does. If you're satisfied with what you've written, click the File menu and then choose the Save option to save all of your work. Give your file a name, and then finally click the Save button.

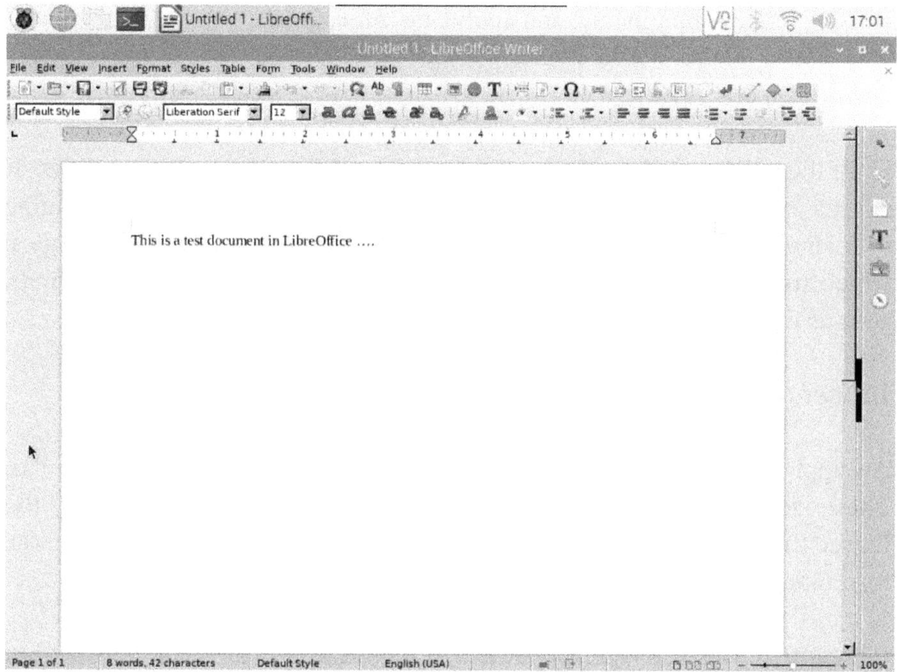

The LibreOffice Writer is one of many programs that you will find in the LibreOffice productivity suite. Other Office programs included in this suite are:

LibreOffice Calc

A spreadsheet program similar to Microsoft Excel used for creating charts and graphs and handling numbers.

LibreOffice Impress

A tool used for creating presentation slides as well as running slideshows, and is similar to Microsoft PowerPoint.

LibreOffice Base

A database management program similar to Microsoft Access and is used for storing, looking up quickly, and analyzing information.

LibreOffice Draw

Is an illustration program where you can create diagrams and pictures. It can act as a vector graphics editor, raster graphics editor, and diagramming tool similar to Microsoft Visio. It provides connectors between shapes, which are available in a range of line styles and facilitates building drawings, such as flowcharts.

LibreOffice Math

An application designed for creating and editing mathematical formulas. These formulas can be incorporated into other documents in the LibreOffice suite, such as those created by Writer or Calc, by embedding the formulas into the document.

LibreOffice uses the OpenDocument standard as its native file format, but supports formats of most other major office suites, including Microsoft Office(example .doc,.xls,ppt, etc), through a variety of import and export filters.

LibreOffice is also made available for other computers as well as operating systems. If you prefer using it on your Pi system, then you can visit libreoffice.org, download the file and then install it on any operating system like Mac OS, or Microsoft Windows.

Task Manager

Sometimes, it may happen that your Pi computer or software does not seem to be responding. But, there is nothing to worry about. This occurs when the computer might be quite busy. To check on this, you can use the Task Manager program on the Pi.

Task Manager

File View Help

CPU usage: 1 % | Memory: 127 MB of 3827 MB used

Command	User	CPU%	RSS	VM-Size	PID
menu-cached	pi	0%	6.4 MB	28.0 MB	837
applet.py	pi	0%	27.2 MB	45.2 MB	813
ssh-agent	pi	0%	292.0 KB	4.4 MB	802
pcmanfm	pi	0%	27.4 MB	112.9 MB	795
lxpanel	pi	0%	28.8 MB	420.9 MB	792
lxpolkit	pi	0%	9.0 MB	46.0 MB	791
openbox	pi	0%	14.8 MB	61.3 MB	788
gvfsd-fuse	pi	0%	6.2 MB	55.4 MB	775

more details Quit

On the top right side, you can see the CPU usage monitor, which will tell you how heavily your Pi's processor is being used. And the right shows the amount of RAM/non-volatile memory being used.

There are two options to open the Task Manager, first by going to the Accessories sub menu in the Application Menu. And secondly, to use the shortcut key, which is by holding down Ctrl and ALT keys and then pressing the Delete key.

If any of the program/s is not responding and you want to terminate it, just right-click in the task list. The menu will appear, and you can choose the Term from it. This option will give a chance to shut down the program safely.

On the other hand, we can also use Kill, but this option will terminate the program immediately and may cause loss of data.

Shutting down the Pi

After exploring the Raspberry Pi OS, it's time to learn how to shut your Raspberry Pi down safely. Like any other computer that people use, the Raspberry Pi stores your files in volatile memory - which is a memory that gets emptied as soon as the system is powered off.

For every document you make, it's important to save as you type, and this is where your files will be transferred to a non-volatile memory, which is the microSD card. But the documents that you're working on aren't the only ones opened. The OS Raspbian has several files opened while running, and if, for any reason, the power cable is pulled from the Raspberry Pi board as the files are still opened, it could lead to the entire OS becoming corrupt. You'll have to install it all over again.

So, to prevent this from occurring, you need to instruct Raspberry Pi OS to power off by selecting the Logout Menu option, which is the last menu item.

Pixel desktop for PC and MAC

The Raspberry Pi Desktop for PCs/laptops was first released in 2016 to remove the barrier to entry for people looking to learn computing. This release is even cheaper than buying a Raspberry Pi because it is free, and you can use it on your existing computer. This makes it easy to get started with this book while waiting for your Raspberry Pi to be shipped to your home.

As the Raspberry Pi Desktop is based on Debian, it can take advantage of the huge bank of amazing free and open source software, programs, games, and other tools from the apt repository. On the Raspberry Pi, you're limited to packages that are compiled to run on ARM chips. However, on the PC image, you have a much wider scope for which packages will run on your machine because Intel chips found in PCs have much greater support.

You can download the PIXEL ISO and write it to a blank DVD or a USB stick. Then you can boot your PC from the disk, and you'll see the PIXEL desktop in no time. You can browse the web, open a programming environment, or use the office suite, all without installing anything on your computer. When you're done, just take out the DVD or USB drive, shut down your computer, and when you power up your computer again, it'll boot back up into your usual OS as before. And once you use the OS a couple of times, you can use the same DVD/USB to install Raspberry Pi desktop on your PC/MAC hard disk

CHAPTER V

Terminal - using the Linux Command Line

Another important part of using a Raspberry Pi is using the terminal application. The terminal is something that a lot of people try to avoid because they feel like it is a bit hard to use. But, after you learn these commands you'll feel really comfortable using the terminal and this is applicable to other Linux operating system.

Understanding the Prompt

You can open the terminal application, by clicking on the Terminal Icon on the task bar, which is placed at the side of the File Manager icon. Or another way is to click on the Terminal application in the Accessories section of the Application Menu.
Once the terminal opens, it shows a prompt that looks like

pi@raspberrypi: ~ $

Here is what the various parts of the promt mean -
pi - it represents the name of the user who is logged in.
raspberrypi - represents the hostname of the machine, this is something that you could have changed as part of the Raspberry Pi configuration application. This is the name the other computers on the network use to identify the Pi.
tilde(~) - The tilde symbol tells the user which directory they are looking at. The tilde is known as the home directory, and this part of the prompt basically shows which directory/folder you are currently working in.
dollar sign($) - This represents the presence of the ordinary user and not the superuser. If the hash (#) symbol is shown instead it means the superuser.

Basic Commands

date - this command displays the system date and time.

pi@raspberrypi:~ $ date
Wed 10 Aug 2022 08:49:44 PM IST

echo - command in Linux is used to display lines of text/string that are passed as an argument. This command is mostly used in shell scripts and batch files to output status text to the screen or a file.

pi@raspberrypi:~ $ echo "Hello! From the Raspberry Pi terminal"
"Hello! From the Raspberry Pi terminal"

Cal - by default this command shows the current month calendar as output. But if you want to see the calendar for the complete year use "cal -y". And if you want to see the calendar for a specific month of the year use cal month year, for example

pi@raspberrypi ~ $ cal 06 2021

```
pi@raspberrypi: ~
File Edit Tabs Help
pi@raspberrypi:~ $ date
Sun 14 Aug 2022 07:12:41 PM IST
pi@raspberrypi:~ $ echo "Hello! From the Raspberry Pi terminal"
Hello! From the Raspberry Pi terminal
pi@raspberrypi:~ $ cal 06 2021
     June 2021
Su Mo Tu We Th Fr Sa
       1  2  3  4  5
 6  7  8  9 10 11 12
13 14 15 16 17 18 19
20 21 22 23 24 25 26
27 28 29 30

pi@raspberrypi:~ $
```

man or --help - To know more about a command and how to use it, use the man command. It shows the manual pages of the command. For example, “man date” shows the manual pages of the date command.

pi@raspberrypi ~ $ man date

To scroll to read the next page use the down arrow key on the keyboard, and to quit and go back press “q” on the keyboard.

Typing in the command name followed by --help shows all the information you need to know about the command.

pi@raspberrypi ~ $ date --help

Navigating the file system

Moving around the filesystem is something we took a look at via the GUI environment using File Manager, and it all looks so easy! But with the terminal, we can do everything, and with great speed and precision. You just need to know the correct commands. If you don’t have permission to perform any of these commands on a particular file or directory, prefacing the command with sudo will probably let you.

pwd - Print working directory
This command will show the full path to the directory you are in, for example typing in pwd once you open the terminal application will show /home/pi/.

pi@raspberrypi:~ $ pwd
/home/pi

ls - List directory content. This command is used to list the contents of a directory.

pi@raspberrypi:~ $ ls
Bookshelf Documents Music Public Videos
Desktop Downloads Pictures Templates

List the files in another directory, such as /var/log

pi@raspberrypi:~ $ ls /var/log

See files and directories in a long list with extra details.

pi@raspberrypi:~ $ ls -l
total 36
drwxr-xr-x 2 pi pi 4096 Aug 14 18:46 Bookshelf
drwxr-xr-x 2 pi pi 4096 Nov 29 2021 Desktop
drwxr-xr-x 4 pi pi 4096 Apr 20 12:32 Documents
drwxr-xr-x 2 pi pi 4096 May 7 2021 Downloads
drwxr-xr-x 2 pi pi 4096 Nov 29 2021 Music
drwxr-xr-x 2 pi pi 4096 May 7 2021 Pictures
drwxr-xr-x 2 pi pi 4096 May 7 2021 Public
drwxr-xr-x 2 pi pi 4096 May 7 2021 Templates
drwxr-xr-x 2 pi pi 4096 May 7 2021 Videos

Like the -l option with ls, there are several more advanced options that you can use with ls, like
-a - The ls command with this option will display all the files. All the files will also include hidden files.
-F - This option will add a symbol beside a filename. It will do this to indicate the file type. If you use this option, you will notice a / after directories names and a * after executable files.
-h - This option is short for human-readable. It expresses file sizes by using kilobytes, megabytes, and gigabytes.
-l - This option will display the result in the long format. It shows the information about the permissions of files, their last modification date,their size.
-m - This option will list the result as a list separated by commas.
-R - This option is the recursive option. It will also list files and directories in the current working directories, open the subdirectories (if any) and list their results too.
-r - It is the reverse option and will display the result in reverse order.
-S - This option will sort the result by their size.
-t - This option will sort the result as per the date and time they were last modified.
-X - This option will sort your result as per the file extension.

With the above option, you can use one option like the command above "ls -l" or multiple options in the same command like "ls -lrt"

cd - Change directory. Using this command we can move around the filesystem. For example, to move from our home directory to Downloads

pi@raspberrypi:~ $ cd Downloads
pi@raspberrypi:~/Downloads $

Move to a directory in another part of the filesystem, for example, /var/log.

pi@raspberrypi:~/Downloads $ cd /var/log
pi@raspberrypi:/var/log $

Go back to the previous directory that we were in.

pi@raspberrypi:/var/log $ cd ..
pi@raspberrypi:/var $

Go back to our home directory.

pi@raspberrypi:/var $ cd ~
pi@raspberrypi:~ $

mkdir filename - creating a directory/folder

pi@raspberrypi:~ $ mkdir testFolder
Once you run this command use the command "ls" to verify if the folder is created. OR you can also open the File Manager to check if the folder is present in the home folder, that is /home/pi

rmdir - remove directory

pi@raspberrypi:~ $ rmdir testFolder
This command will remove only an empty directory. Once you run this command use the command "ls" to verify if the folder is deleted. OR you can also open the File Manager to check if the folder is deleted in the home

folder, that is /home/pi

pi@raspberrypi:~ $ rm -R fullFolder
The -R option helps to remove non-empty directories. If you rm the command without the -R option, when the folder is not empty, you will get an error saying “”rmdir: failed to remove ‘fullFolder/’: Directory not empty.”

Working with files

In addition to creating new files, sometimes we need to take a peek inside a file and look for a specific string, error or bug, and with these commands, we can do all this from the terminal.

touch - used to create a file without any content

pi@raspberrypi:~ $ touch testFile.txt

less - Print files to the terminal
This command will print the contents of a file in sections and we can scroll through the file using the arrow keys, Page Up / Down and Home / End. And press “q” key on the keyboard to quit.

pi@raspberrypi:~ $ less /var/log/syslog

Tail - prints the last 10 lines of the specified files, if more than one file name is provided then data from each file is preceded by its filename.

pi@raspberrypi:~ $ tail /var/log/syslog

cp - Copying files and folders from one location to another

pi@raspberrypi:~ $ cp testFile.txt ~/Documents
This will copy the testFile.txt from the current folder to the Documents folder of Pi. To check if the file is copied over “cd Documents” and then give the command “ls”, you should see a copy of testFile.txt in the Documents folder.

mv - Instead of making a copy of the file, if you want to move it from one place to another

pi@raspberrypi:~ $ mv /home/pi/testFile.txt /home/pi/Desktop
This will move the testFile.txt to the desktop, you can verify this using the File Manager, or "cd /home/pi/Desktop" followed by the "ls" command.

rm - to delete files

pi@raspberrypi:~ $ rm testFile.txt
This deletes the file, and like the mkdir command there is no output, you will have to type "ls" if you want to double check if the file is deleted. Remember you have moved the file in the previous command to the desktop, so create a new file using the command "touch testFile.txt"

nano is an easy-to-use text editor that is installed by default in Raspberry Pi operating system and many other Linux distributions.You can run nano by just typing in nano at the command prompt.

pi@raspberrypi:~ $ nano testFile.txt
Nano will follow the path and open that file if it exists. If it does not exist, it'll start a new buffer with that file name in that directory.

At the top row, you'll see the name of the program version number (GNU nano 3.2), the name and extension of the file you're editing(testFile.txt), and whether the file has been modified since it was last saved. If you have a new file that isn't saved yet, you'll see "New Buffer."

Next, you'll see the contents of your file, where you can start typing.

Lastly, the final two rows at the bottom are the shortcut lines. Program functions are referred to as "shortcuts" in nano, such as saving, quitting, searching, etc. The most common ones are listed at the bottom of the screen, but there are many more that aren't shown here.

Once you are done working on your text file and you want to save it and exit nano. This is executed by pressing Ctrl+x.Nano will ask you if you want to save the changes, you can type:
Y, then Enter – to save all your changes
N, then Enter- to cancel any changes
Try also using the shortcuts in nano, you can try cutting(ctrl+k) and pasting(ctrl+u), searching(ctrl+w), saving file without exiting (ctrl+o) and many more. If you are looking for more help use the "man nano" command.

cat - Print files to the terminal. lt reads data from the file and gives its content as output. It helps us to create, view, and concatenate files

pi@raspberrypi:~ $ cat testFile.txt
Hi, this is some text....

Print contents of the file to the terminal with line numbers, this is ideal if you need to explain a python program to your friend.
pi@raspberrypi:~ $ cat -n testFile.txt
1 Hi, this is some text....
2

grep - filter searches a file for a particular pattern of characters, and displays all lines that contain that pattern. The pattern that is searched in the file is referred to as the regular expression (grep stands for global search for regular expression and print out).

pi@raspberrypi:~ $ grep -i 'Some TEXT' testFile.txt
Hi, this is ***some text****....*

The -i option enables grep to search for the "Some TEXT" string case insensitively in the given file. Like ls there are multiple options you can use, to learn more about these options you can use "man grep" command.

pi@raspberrypi:~ $ grep -ci 'Some TEXT' testFile.txt
1

The -c option allows user to match the number of lines that matches the given string "Some TEXT"

sudo

sudo is a widely used command in the Linux command line, sudo stands for "SuperUser Do". So, if you want any command to be done with administrative or root privileges, you can use sudo as a prefix.

Using wildcards

If a directory contains a lot of files with similar filenames and if you want to delete a group of such files, you don't need to repeat the command by typing out each filename.Using wildcards will make your life easy, by having to type the command only once.

?(single character) - pic?.jpg - This means that the files start with a pic and have exactly one character after it before the extension starts.
(any number of characters) - *pic - in this case any files that have the word pic in it are selected for the operation.
[...](wildcard will match any one of the characters in bracket)- [xyz]* - in this scenario all the files that start with the letter x,y or z.
[^...](opposite of the above)-[^xyz]* - in this scenario the files selected should not have the letter start with x, y or z.

Now, consider a scenario where you want to delete all the photos you downloaded from the camera to your picture folder, you can do it in one command using the * wildcard -

rm /home/pi/Pictures/pic.jpg*

Pipes and Redirection

Pipes are simply a way of chaining two programs together, so the output of one can serve as the input to another.

pi@raspberrypi:~ $ ls -la | less
Press "q" on your keyboard, to exit the less program, and use up/down the arrow keys to scroll up/dowm.

pi@raspberrypi:~ $ lscpu | grep 'MHz'
CPU max MHz: 1500.0000
CPU min MHz: 600.0000
In this example we use lscpu to print the details of the CPU which is passed via a pipe | to grep which we instruct to look for "MHz".

Redirecting means you can send the results from a command to a file instead of showing the output on the screen. Use the > (greater-than) sign along with the file name, to which you would like to send the output..

pi@raspberrypi:~ $ ls -l > directoryList.txt
This sends the output of the ls commands and writes it into the directoryList.txt file.

pi@raspberrypi ~ $ cat testFile.txt directoryList.txt > thirdFile.txt
Another situation to use a redirect, is to concatenate two files and send their output to the third file. To check if the command ran successfully run "cat thirdFile.txt"

File Permissions

Raspberry Pi OS is a Linux based OS, which means it is a multi-user OS which can be accessed by many users simultaneously. So it has to have security to prevent people from accessing each other's confidential files.

When you execute an "ls -l" command, you are given information about the security of the files on the left most side of the terminal

pi@raspberrypi:~ $ ls -l testFile.txt
-rw-r--r-- 1 pi pi 27 Aug 14 20:56 testFile.txt

- The first character will almost always be either a '-', which means it's a file, or a 'd', which means it's a directory.
- The next nine characters (rw-r--r--) show the security, which is something we are going to discuss in detail below.
- The next column shows the owner of the file. In this case it is Pi, this is the user we have logged into the Pi in.
- The next column shows the group owner of the file. Which is Pi.
- The next column shows the size of the file in bytes. Which is 27 bytes.
- The next column shows the date and time the file was last modified. That is Aug 14 20:56.
- And, the last column gives the filename, which is testFile.txt.

There are nine characters in three sets of three characters, in the leftmost section of the ls -l output. Each of the three can have "rwx" characters that refer to a different operation you can perform on the file.
--- --- ---
rwx rwx rwx
user group other
The **'r'** means you can "read" the file's contents.
'w' means you can "write", or modify, the file's contents.
And **'x'** means you can "execute" the file. This permission is given only if the file is a program.

If any of the "rwx" characters is replaced by a '-', then that permission has been revoked.

user – The user permissions apply only to the owner of the file or directory, they will not impact the actions of other users.
group – The group permissions apply only to the group that has been assigned to the file or directory, they will not affect the actions of other users.
others – The others permissions apply to all other users on the system, this

is the permission group that you want to watch the most.

Based on the output of ls -l, the user's permissions for some files is "rw-" as the first three characters. This means that the owner of the file ("pi", i.e. you) can "read" it (look at its contents) and "write" it (modify its contents). You cannot execute it because it is not a program; it is a text file.

If "r-x" is the second set of 3 characters it means that the members of the group "pi" can only read and execute the files.

Changing security permissions

chmod - use to change the security permissions. "chmod", which stands for "change mode", because the nine security characters are collectively called the security "mode" of the file.

The first argument you give to the "chmod" command is 'u', 'g', 'o'. That is:

- u for user
- g for group
- o for others

After this use

- a '+' for adding
- a '-' for removing
- and a "=" for assigning a permission.

Then specify the permission r,w or x you want to change. Here also you can use a combination of r,w,x.

pi@raspberrypi:~ $ sudo chmod u+x testFile.txt
pi@raspberrypi:~ $ ls -l testFile.txt
-rwxr--r-- 1 pi pi 27 Aug 14 20:56 testFile.txt

Here though this is a text file, for testing we can give the user an execute permission using "u+x".

You can also change multiple permissions at once.

sudo chmod ug=rx,o+r abc.py
assigns read(r) and execute(x) permission to both user(u) and group(g) and add read permission to others for the file abc.py.

Another variation to assigning permission using chmod is using the octal notation. You will have to follow the table -

Number	Permission Type	Symbol
0	No Permission	—
1	Execute	–x
2	Write	-w-
3	Execute + Write	-wx
4	Read	r–
5	Read + Execute	r-x
6	Read +Write	rw-
7	Read + Write +Execute	rwx

Using the octal notations table instead of ‘r’, ‘w’ and ‘x’. Each digit octal notation can be used in either of the group ‘u’,’g’,’o’.

sudo chmod ugo+rwx anotherFile.txt
is the same as
sudo chmod 777 anotherFile.txt

Similarly
sudo chmod u=r,g=wx,o=rx testFile.txt
is the same as

sudo chmod 435 testFile.txt

chown- is a command used to change owners, which is self-explanatory. While chmod handles what users can do with a file once they have access to it, chown assigns ownership. As you may have noticed, none of the chmod commands we discussed above changed who owns the files we're working with. That's where chown comes in.

sudo chown someotheruser learningnotes.txt
sudo chown othergroup learningnotes.txt

Remember if you change the owner of the file to someone else you may not have access to the file any more. And will see a permission denied when you try and open the file.

Updating and Upgrading and installing

When you know your way around the command line, downloading and installing new software on your Pi or any computer running the Linux OS is quite easy. Linux distribution like the Raspberry Pi OS which is based on Debian distribution has a large database of available software in its repository. This provides a one-stop shop for everything you might need, and you can think of this as a text-based app store.

The software comes in what are called packages, which are software programs that can be downloaded from the Internet and installed simply by typing a command in the prompt. To download and install these packages, you normally use a package manager, which downloads and installs not only the software you requested, but also all other related required software, known as dependencies. The Raspbian distribution uses a package manager called apt.

To manage your software, you need the authorization of the administrator, who is known as the superuser (sudo).

To install software, you'll first want to make sure Raspbian's list of software sources is up to date by running the following command. And remember you need to be connected to the Internet for this command to work.

pi@raspberrypi:~ $ sudo apt update

Hit:1 http://raspbian.raspberrypi.org/raspbian buster InRelease
Hit:2 http://archive.raspberrypi.org/debian buster InRelease
Reading package lists... Done
Building dependency tree
Reading state information... Done
176 packages can be upgraded. Run 'apt list --upgradable' to see them.

The sudo part of the command means you're running this as a root user, so you'll be prompted to enter a password. The next word, apt, is the name of the package manager, and update tells the package manager what to do, which in this case is to update its list of software. This command updates the list of available package versions that your package manager is aware of. (The package manager keeps such a list in the Raspberry's file system.). And after you hit Enter to run the command, you should see text scrolls by, giving you information about the newest listings.

Once you've done that, you can **install** a program with the following

pi@raspberrypi:~ $ sudo apt install firefox-esr
In this command, firefox-esr is the name of the package you want to install Morzilla Firefox internet browser. And once the installation is complete you should see the Firefox browser under the internet section of the Application Menu.

If you aren't sure of the name, you can search the repository by running, for example in this case you know Morzilla's internet browser is called Firefox, so you will tend to search with the keyword Firefox

pi@raspberrypi:~ $ sudo apt-cache search firefox

To **upgrade** your existing software, run the command sudo apt update first, then run

pi@raspberrypi:~ $sudo apt upgrade

sudo apt update updates the list of available package versions but doesn't install or upgrade any of them, whereas sudo apt upgrade updates the packages themselves, checking the list to do so. For this reason, you should always run update before upgrade.

You can **remove an application**, in this case the Morzilla Firefox browser, with the command

pi@raspberrypi:~ $sudo apt remove firefox-esr
This command leaves behind files that are somehow related to the software, such as configuration files and logs. If you don't intend to use those files in any way, you can remove everything by using purge

sudo apt-get purge firefox-esr

Warning : Do not remove any package that you didn't install yourself unless you're absolutely certain that you know what it's for. It may be a necessary package that comes with the Raspberry Pi OS, and removing it may lead to a system crash.

CHAPTER VI

Must Try Application on the Pi

Raspberry Pi is undoubtedly an excellent little device whose importance is rising with each coming day. An OS is incomplete without the apps. Though there are tons of apps, as a beginner finding the best apps to install on Raspberry Pi can be a challenge.

Raspberry Pi OS comes with a default set of applications, some of which we discussed in Chapter IV. Here are a few more applications which help you perform tasks like programming, taking a break to play games, listening to music, watching movies, etc.

Scratch

Scratch is an easy to use block-based visual programming software that can run on a Raspberry Pi locally, and if you are connected to the internet, you can use the Chrome browser on any OS by going to https://scratch.mit.edu/.

Using Scratch, you can create your very own animations, games, and more using a straightforward drag-and-drop interface.

To get to Scratch locally on the Raspberry Pi, click the Programming sub menu in the Application menu and select Scratch 3, which is the latest version of Scratch.

To say that Scratch is not a powerful programming language misses the point, which is that it is a friendly environment for creating and making things happen quickly. A young programmer can see the blocks of code highlighted as they're executed, and blocks can be changed and the effects seen in real-time.

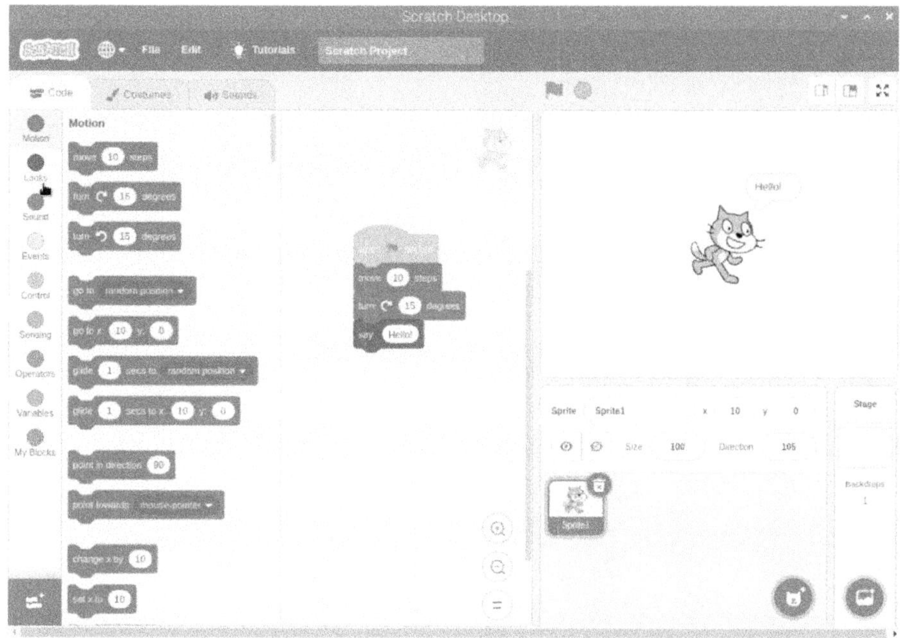

Scratch programs are aimed at manipulating sprites on a stage. There's a large community of Scratch users, and the ability to share sprites and code with the community is baked right into the platform.

For some history, Scratch was developed and launched in May 2007 by the MIT Media Lab's Lifelong Kindergarten group as a new way of teaching programming to young people. And their mission was to spread creative, caring, collaborative, and equitable approaches to coding and learning around the world. Providing young people with digital tools and opportunities to imagine, create, share, and learn.

Thonny Python IDE

An IDE (Integrated Development Environment) contains all the features in just one software. So you can focus on writing code, which is the most important thing you can do. The Thonny IDE will allow you to be more productive when writing Python programs. Also, when you begin programming, using an IDE is great because you don't have to think about all the configurations. You can just start and learn step by step by directly programming.

To get to Thonny Python IDE on the Pi, click the Programming sub menu in the Application Menu and select Thonny Python IDE.

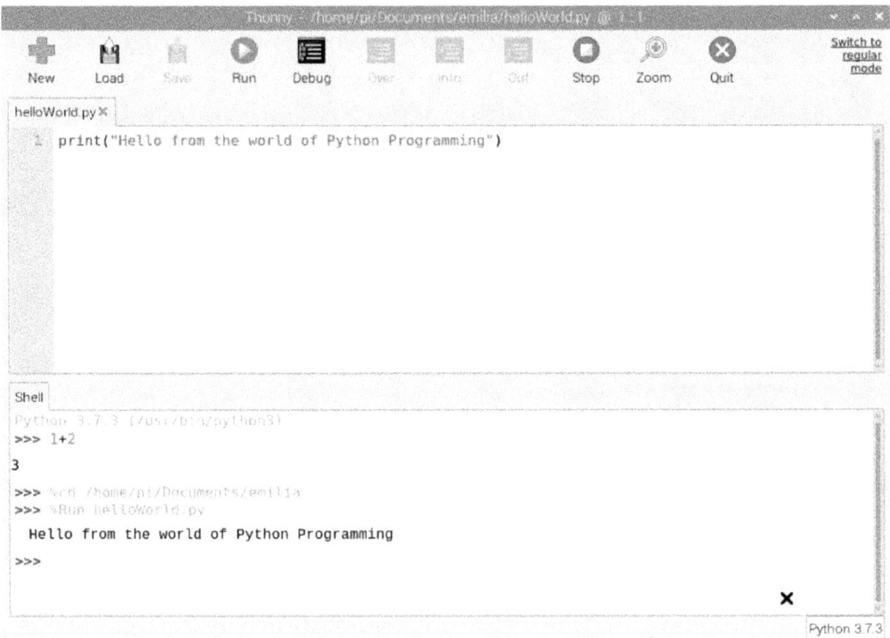

Here are the features of Thonny Python IDE, and reasons for using an IDE if you're just getting started with Python programming

- Has language support such as auto completion, syntax highlighting, etc.
- Run programs with the output shown on the same screen.
- Save your programs, open them and edit them.
- Debug your programs so you can see what's happening during the execution.

All the features of Thonny Python IDE are going to be discussed in detail in Chapter VIII

Sonic Pi

If you are into creating your own music, you should try Sonic Pi. It is another programming language provided by the Raspberry Pi Foundation which is mainly used for creating music. You can also find it under the Programming section of the Application menu. It is a live coding environment based on Ruby programming language, originally designed to support both computing and music lessons in schools. It was developed by Sam Aaron in the University of Cambridge Computer Laboratory in collaboration with the Raspberry Pi Foundation.

Sense Hat emulator

This application emulates the Raspberry Pi Sense HAT. An interactive application is provided to permit manipulation of the emulated sensors like temperature, humidity, pressure, orientation, etc., along with command line utilities for recording and playing back sensor readings from an actual HAT.

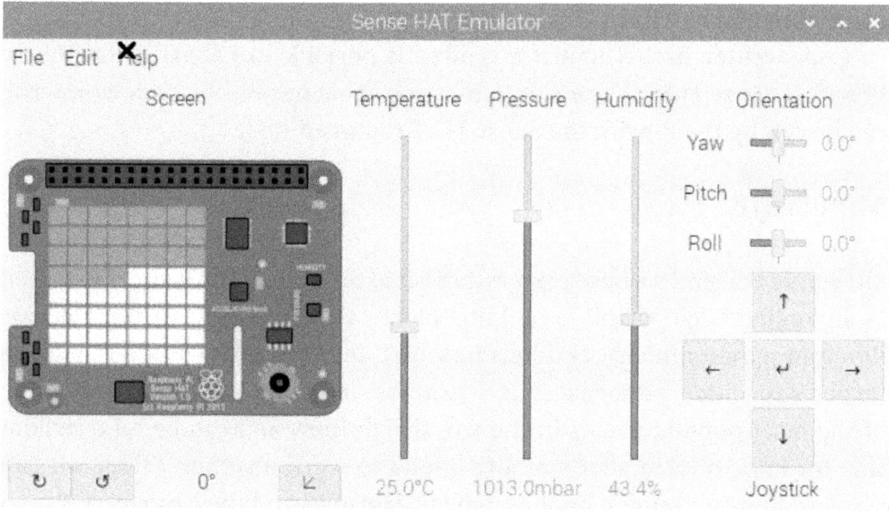

Now, if you are wondering what a Sense HAT is and why do we need an emulator ?

Sense HAT is an add-on board for Raspberry Pi, made especially for the Astro Pi Mission to space. It was launched by the International Space Station in December 2015, which offered young people the amazing opportunity to conduct scientific investigations in space by writing computer programs that run on Raspberry Pi computers aboard the International Space Station (ISS).

- The Sense HAT has an 8×8 RGB LED matrix, a five-button joystick and includes the following sensors:
- Gyroscope
- Accelerometer
- Magnetometer
- Temperature
- Barometric pressure
- Humidity

While the Sense HAT has temperature, pressure and humidity sensors and can change its behaviour according to changing environmental conditions around it. The Sense HAT emulator has sliders you can move to change these values, so you can test how your code responds to environmental variables.

Code written in this emulator is directly portable to a physical Raspberry Pi with a Sense HAT without modification. This means any code you write can be run by the Pi with the Sense HAT mounted on it.

Minecraft

Minecraft is a game where players can build anything. The game, described as an ‘online Lego’, involves building blocks and creating structures across different environments and terrains. Set in a virtual world, the game involves resource gathering, crafting items, building, and combat. It’s one of the most popular games in the world right now and can be an excellent way for kids to learn about creativity and to work together. Minecraft can be played on computers, phones, tablets, consoles and the Raspberry Pi.

On Raspberry Pi OS, this game can be found in the games section of the Application menu. In addition to playing the game regularly, with Minecraft for Pi you can also learn how to control the player, manually build with blocks and use the Python interface to manipulate the world around you.

Pinta

Pinta is an open-source, cross-platform bitmap image drawing and editing program inspired by Paint.NET, a similar image editing program which is limited to Microsoft Windows. Pinta has more features than Microsoft Paint. Compared with open-source image editor GIMP, Pinta is simpler and has fewer features.

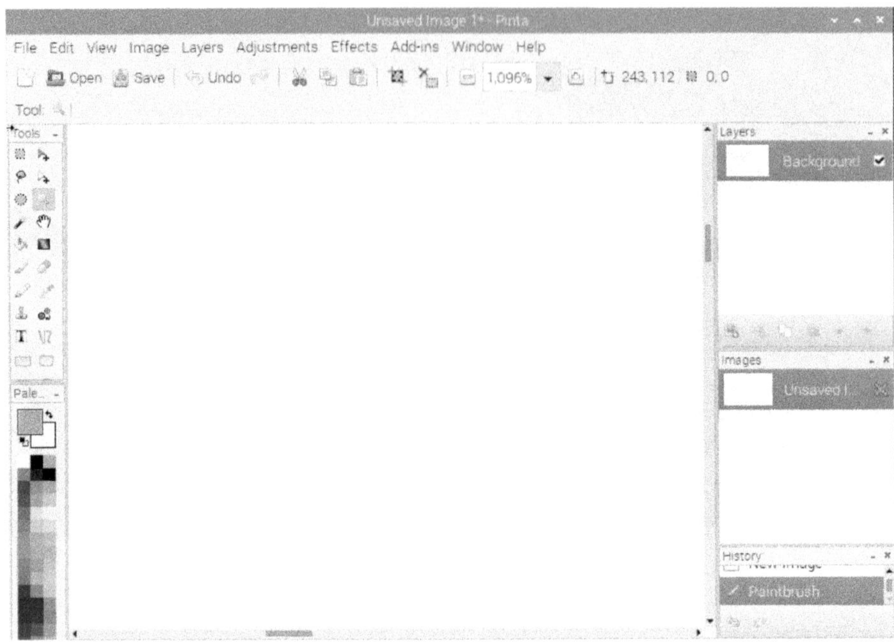

Unlike some simple image editing software, Pinta also features support for image layers. The tool's focus is on usability, which is reflected in several of the program's main features like unlimited undo history, multiple language support and flexible toolbar arrangement, including floating as windows or docking around the image edge.

You can launch it by clicking on Pinta from the Graphics section of the Application menu.

GIMP

GIMP is an acronym for GNU Image Manipulation Program. It is a freely distributed program for such tasks as photo retouching, image composition and image authoring.

It is not designed to be used for drawing, though some artists and creators have used it for such. GIMP, as a fully functioning image editor, rivals other industry standard software such as Adobe Photoshop and Corel Paint Shop Pro in terms of features such as multiple layers, the ability to resize and re-shape images, cropping, colour manipulation, and so on.

The command used to install GIMP using apt command is given below, and this will take a few minutes. Or you can also install it from the Recommended Software application which is under the Preferences section of the Application menu

pi@raspberrypi: ~ $ sudo apt install gimp

To run the GIMP application on your Raspberry Pi, you will need to enter the name "gimp" in the Terminal, and it will successfully appear on your screen in a few seconds.

pi@raspberrypi: ~ $ gimp

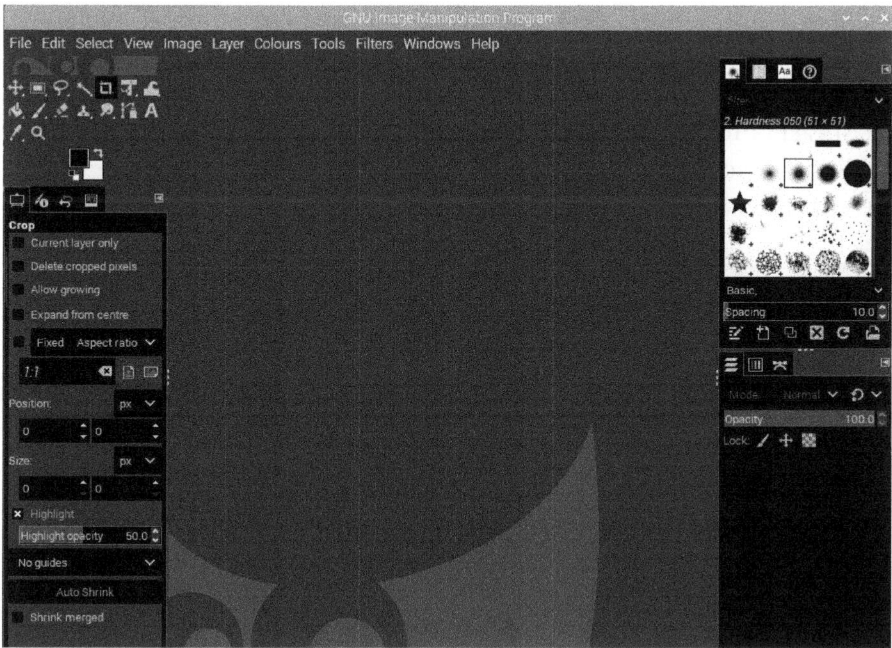

The current look of GIMP consists of 2 main windows - the image window and a toolbox. Also, by default, there's another utility window. The image window is always under the utility windows, but can quickly go over using the Tab key. In GIMP, a single-window option is included, which docks the utilities onto the screen.

VLC media player

If you enjoy listening to music and watching movies, you need a versatile music or video player for the Raspberry Pi. VLC on your Raspberry Pi desktop is the best application for this. The VLC media player is a free, open-source, portable, cross-platform media player software and streaming media server developed by the VideoLAN project. VLC is available for desktop OS, Microsoft Windows, macOS, Linux and mobile platforms, such as Android, iOS and iPadOS.

VLC player accepts media and music files in commonly used formats such as av, mkv, mp4, mp3,ogg, etc. If you have gone through Chapter II in detail, you have realised that the Raspberry Pi does not have a speaker. So to enjoy a movie or your music playlist, you will have to connect a set of speakers to the audio jack or connect your speakers via Bluetooth. In addition, if your monitor comes with speakers, you can play music via the HDMI cable.

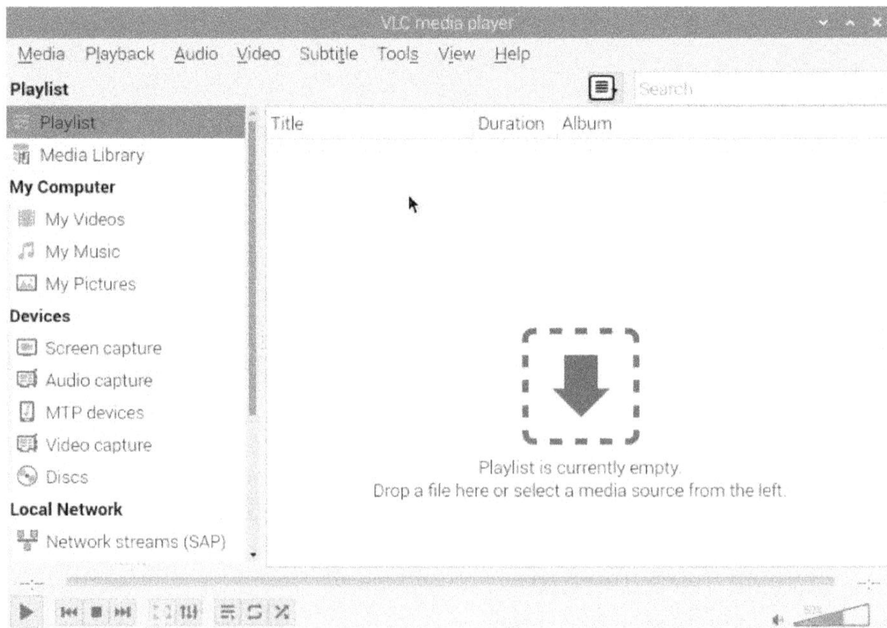

And to run the VLC media player on your Pi, you will need to enter the name “vlc” in the Terminal, and it will successfully appear on your screen in a few seconds. OR, you can launch it from the Sound & Video section of the Application menu.

Bookshelf

This is an application to browse and download Raspberry Pi Press titles. Bookshelf shows the entire current catalogue of free magazines, that is, The MagPi, HackSpace and Wireframe, with a complete set of back issues. And all the free books published from Raspberry Pi Press.

To launch Bookshelf application go to the Help section of the Application menu. When you run the application, it automatically updates the catalogue if you are connected to the internet and shows any new titles which have been released since you last ran.

You can right-click and download the book or magazine to read it offline.

Claws Mail

The Raspberry Pi OS comes with an open-source email program called Claws Mail. It is pre-installed, and you can find it in the Internet section of the Application menu.

Following are some prerequisites if you want to use email on Raspberry Pi -

- For sending emails, you need to know the details of the server. You can find this information on the website of your email provider.
- Your email user ID and password should be the same as you use when logging on with webmail.

To launch Claws mail client, go to the Internet section of the Application menu. To use Claws mail for sending and receiving emails, first you need to add an account from the configuration wizard of Claws mail. Apart from adding a new account, you can also edit the account settings and delete an account by using the Configuration menu.

Once you are done with Configuration, go to the top left and click the Get Mail button. It will show your mail folder on the left and messages on the right at the top.

To read the messages, you can use two methods. One is to use the message preview pane at the bottom right, and the other is to double-click on a message to open in its own window. There is a Menu bar across the top of Claws mail for composing a new message, replying, and forwarding a message. This is a very simple mail client when compared to something like Microsoft Outlook.

CHAPTER VII

Connecting and Viewing the Pi Remotely

Networking is vital for many Raspberry Pi projects, such as home automation, and being connected to the internet can make learning a bit easier. The Raspberry Pi 4 has 2 network interfaces to connect to the internet that is Ethernet port and Wi-Fi. The Ethernet is called eth0, and the Wi-Fi is wlan0. You will have to remember these names as you need to use them with some of the commands below.

In this Chapter, you will learn about connecting the Pi to the internet and how to control it through the power of networking from another computer/ laptop.

Getting IP address and checking connectivity to the internet

ifconfig - stands for "interface configuration." It is used to view and change the configuration of the network interfaces on your system.

```
pi@raspberrypi:~ $ ifconfig
eth0: flags=4099<UP,BROADCAST,MULTICAST> mtu 1500
ether e4:5f:01:60:fd:ad txqueuelen 1000 (Ethernet)
RX packets 0 bytes 0 (0.0 B)
RX errors 0 dropped 0 overruns 0 frame 0
TX packets 0 bytes 0 (0.0 B)
TX errors 0 dropped 0 overruns 0 carrier 0 collisions 0
    lo: flags=73<UP,LOOPBACK,RUNNING> mtu 65536
inet 127.0.0.1 netmask 255.0.0.0
inet6 ::1 prefixlen 128 scopeid 0x10<host>
loop txqueuelen 1000 (Local Loopback)
RX packets 16 bytes 960 (960.0 B)
RX errors 0 dropped 0 overruns 0 frame 0
TX packets 16 bytes 960 (960.0 B)
TX errors 0 dropped 0 overruns 0 carrier 0 collisions 0
    wlan0: flags=4163<UP,BROADCAST,RUNNING,MULTICAST> mtu 1500
inet 10.10.10.6 netmask 255.255.255.0 broadcast 10.10.10.255
```

inet6 fe80::1b47:4a8f:b6b6:e799 prefixlen 64 scopeid 0x20<link>
ether e4:5f:01:60:fd:ae txqueuelen 1000 (Ethernet)
RX packets 489873 bytes 685539755 (653.7 MiB)
RX errors 0 dropped 0 overruns 0 frame 0
TX packets 218778 bytes 20582847 (19.6 MiB)
TX errors 0 dropped 0 overruns 0 carrier 0 collisions 0

Here, eth0, lo and wlan0 are the names of the active network interfaces on the system

- eth0 is the first Ethernet interface. This interface will show an ip address if a LAN cable is connected to the Pi ethernet port.
- lo is the loopback interface. The system uses this special network interface to communicate with itself. And the default IP address for the port is 127.0.0.1.
- wlan0 is the name of the first wireless network interface on the Pi and based on the output of the command above, the IP address is 10.10.10.06.

If you've found the output too long and know you're connected to WiFi, you can use the following command to get the IP address of your Pi.

pi@raspberrypi:~ $ ifconfig wlan0
wlan0: flags=4163<UP,BROADCAST,RUNNING,MULTICAST> mtu 1500
inet ***10.10.10.6*** *netmask 255.255.255.0 broadcast 10.10.10.255*
inet6 fe80::1b47:4a8f:b6b6:e799 prefixlen 64 scopeid 0x20<link>
ether e4:5f:01:60:fd:ae txqueuelen 1000 (Ethernet)
RX packets 590644 bytes 827447946 (789.1 MiB)
RX errors 0 dropped 0 overruns 0 frame 0
TX packets 262258 bytes 24521590 (23.3 MiB)
TX errors 0 dropped 0 overruns 0 carrier 0 collisions 0

When a network interface is active, it can send and receive data. When it is inactive, it cannot transmit or receive. You can use ifconfig to change the status of a network interface from inactive to active or vice versa. To enable an inactive interface, provide ifconfig with the interface name followed by the keyword up.

pi@raspberrypi:~ $sudo ifconfig wlan0 up

And to disable an active network interface use the down keyword.

pi@raspberrypi:~ $sudo ifconfig wlan0 down

hostname -I - if you need your IP address in a single line, use the command.

pi@raspberrypi:~ $ hostname -I
10.10.10.6

ping- command is used to check the network connectivity between host and server/host. This command takes as input the IP address or the URL and sends a data packet to the specified address with the message "PING" and gets a response from the server/host. This time is recorded, which is called latency, fast ping low latency means faster connection

pi@raspberrypi:~ $ ping google.com
PING google.com (142.250.192.14) 56(84) bytes of data.
64 bytes from bom12s14-in-f14.1e100.net (142.250.192.14): icmp_seq=1 ttl=52 time=672 ms
64 bytes from bom12s14-in-f14.1e100.net (142.250.192.14): icmp_seq=2 ttl=52 time=565 ms
64 bytes from bom12s14-in-f14.1e100.net (142.250.192.14): icmp_seq=3 ttl=52 time=308 ms
64 bytes from bom12s14-in-f14.1e100.net (142.250.192.14): icmp_seq=4 ttl=52 time=192 ms
64 bytes from bom12s14-in-f14.1e100.net (142.250.192.14): icmp_seq=5 ttl=52 time=275 ms
64 bytes from bom12s14-in-f14.1e100.net (142.250.192.14): icmp_seq=6 ttl=52 time=317 ms
^C
--- google.com ping statistics ---
6 packets transmitted, 6 received, 0% packet loss, time 98ms
rtt min/avg/max/mdev = 192.364/388.172/672.162/170.708 ms

To stop pinging, we should use ctrl+c otherwise it will keep sending packets.
from - It tells the target and its IP address, which is 142.250.192.14. Any website's IP address might differ depending on our geographical location.

ttl=52 - It tells the value, that is, time to live from 1-255. Also, it indicates the network number of hops a packet could take before any router removes it.
icmp_seq=1 - It tells all ICMP(Internet Control Message Protocol) packet's sequence numbers. It increases by a single number for all subsequent echo requests. Ping uses ICMP to send an ICMP echo message to the specified host, and if the host is available, it then sends ICMP a reply message back.
time=672 ms - It tells the time it took any packet to reach the target and come back to the origin. It is expressed in ms (milliseconds).

Now if you know another computer/Pi's IP address in the network you can use the same command with the IP address instead of the google.com. With google.com we are checking if the Pi is connected to the internet via your WiFi router.

pi@raspberrypi:~ $ping 10.10.10.5

ping localhost - Here, the name localhost will refer to your Pi, and when we enter this command, we say - ping your own system. Since the localhost IP address is 127.0.0.1, you can also use ping 127.0.0.1

pi@raspberrypi:~ $ ping localhost

Configure WiFi from the Terminal

Raspi-config

If you have not configured your WiFi networking using the Wifi icon on the taskbar, you can also do it via the command line using raspi-config. It is handy when running a bare minimum install of the Raspberry Pi OS for a project without the PIXEL desktop (this is called the Raspberry Pi OS lite).

As you learned in Chapter V, raspi-config is a console-based application used to configure various settings on your Pi. It can also be used for network configuration in setting up your WiFi details, mentioned below.

pi@raspberrypi:~ $ sudo raspi-config

Select Wi-fi, then follow the on-screen instructions to enter your network's SSID, followed by the password. When you're done, select "Finish" on the main menu to close

Finally, reboot your Pi using the command "*sudo reboot*" to apply the settings you just changed. You should be connected to WiFi after your Pi reboots.

Manually updating using WPA Supplicant

This is the least easy option as it will involve some typing. For this, you will have to update the wpa_supplicant.conf file. The wireless configuration on the Pi is located in /etc/wpa_supplicant. You will have to use nano to edit the configuration file

pi@raspberrypi:~ $ sudo nano /etc/wpa_supplicant/wpa_supplicant.conf

At the bottom of the file, type the following information -

```
ctrl_interface=DIR=/var/run/wpa_supplicant GROUP=netdev
update_config=1
country=IN
network={
ssid="YOURSSID"
psk="YOURPASSWORD"
key_mgmt=WPA-PSK
}
```

Once you save and quit out of the nano editor, it is a good idea to reboot the Pi using "sudo reboot" for the WiFi configuration to take effect.

For some reason, if this does not work, first check if your WiFi network is detected by the Pi using the following command

pi@raspberrypi:~ $ sudo iwlist wlan0 scan

And also double check/retype your password in the wpa_supplicant.conf file using nano.

Setting up a Static IP address

For some Pi projects, you will need to configure a static IP address for your Pi, which means an IP address that always remains the same for the Pi. This is handy if you have multiple Pi's in your network and are running them headless, without a keyboard, mouse and monitor.

To set up a static IP address, you will need to modify the dhcpcd.conf file. DHCP (Dynamic Host Configuration Protocol) is a network protocol used to automate the process of giving a device IP address in a network. Basically, DHCP is the protocol responsible for giving your Pi and other computers on your network IP address from the WiFi router.

Before setting up the static IP, we need to figure out the DNS (Domain Naming System) server IP address using the command

pi@raspberrypi:~ $ sudo nano /etc/resolv.conf

The file will have an entry like, make a note of the NAMESERVER_IP.

 # Generated by resolvconf
nameserver 10.10.10.254

Now, to setup a static IP for your Pi and ignore DHCP, use the nano editor to open the file

pi@raspberrypi:~ $ sudo nano /etc/dhcpcd.conf

Then add the following section at the bottom of the file

interface wlan0
static ip_address=YOUR_PI_IP/24
static routers=ROUTER_IP
static domain_name_servers=NAMESERVER_IP

It is a good idea first to know what is YOUR_PI_IP address that your are using. For this use the command we learnt earlier "*hostname -I*".

Once you save and exit from the nano editor, it is a good idea to reboot the Pi using the command "*sudo reboot*".

Manually shutting down your network.

If for some reason you have to shutdown Pi WiFi or ethernet network, you can use the commands below. It is always a good idea to disable the Wi-Fi interface if you are not using it in your project.

pi@raspberrypi:~ $ sudo ifdown wlan0

And to start the network you can use

pi@raspberrypi:~ $ sudo ifup wlan0

For the ethernet network replace wlan0 with eth0. And these commands also come in handy instead of rebooting your Pi, as we did previously.

Connecting to Pi from another Computer via SSH

To connect to the Pi remotely from another computer on the network, you will have to use SSH. SSH stands for Secure Shell. It allows you to remotely connect to a server or system like the Pi from another device using encrypted communications. The primary benefit of SSH is the encryption itself. A hacker can sniff out communications and log things like usernames and passwords. Since SSH is encrypted, that's no longer possible.

To access the Pi on another computer, you will need to enable the SSH option in the Raspberry Pi OS and you can do this in multiple ways. You can use the Raspberry Pi configuration tool from the Prefrences section of the application menu, and then go to the interfaces tab and click on the Enable radio button.

Another way of doing this is using the Terminal - use the command "sudo raspi-config" and then go to the Interface Options and select the SSH option.

pi@raspberrypi:~ $ sudo raspi-config

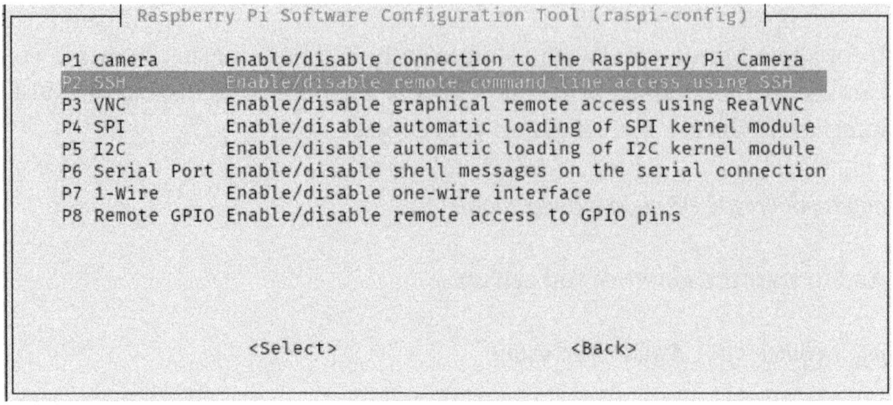

```
Raspberry Pi Software Configuration Tool (raspi-config)

P1 Camera      Enable/disable connection to the Raspberry Pi Camera
P2 SSH         Enable/disable remote command line access using SSH
P3 VNC         Enable/disable graphical remote access using RealVNC
P4 SPI         Enable/disable automatic loading of SPI kernel module
P5 I2C         Enable/disable automatic loading of I2C kernel module
P6 Serial Port Enable/disable shell messages on the serial connection
P7 1-Wire      Enable/disable one-wire interface
P8 Remote GPIO Enable/disable remote access to GPIO pins

               <Select>                    <Back>
```

Which will prompt - “Would you like the SSH server to be enabled?” choose “Yes.” Press Enter again at the confirmation box, “The SSH server is enabled. Navigate down and select “Finish.”

Also if you don’t know the IP address of your Pi, make a note of it using the command we learnt earlier

pi@raspberrypi:~ $ hostname -I
10.10.10.2

Now from your laptop/computer you should be able to SSH into the Pi. If you are using a Mac or Linux computer, you can use the Terminal app, and if you are using Microsoft Windows, you will have to use an SSH client app like Putty which you will have to download from the internet. Type the following command

ssh pi@10.10.10.2

You’ll see a warning the first time, type Yes and press Enter. Once done, you will be prompted for the password of Pi user, type it in and press Enter. On successful login, you’ll be presented with the Terminal prompt of your Pi.

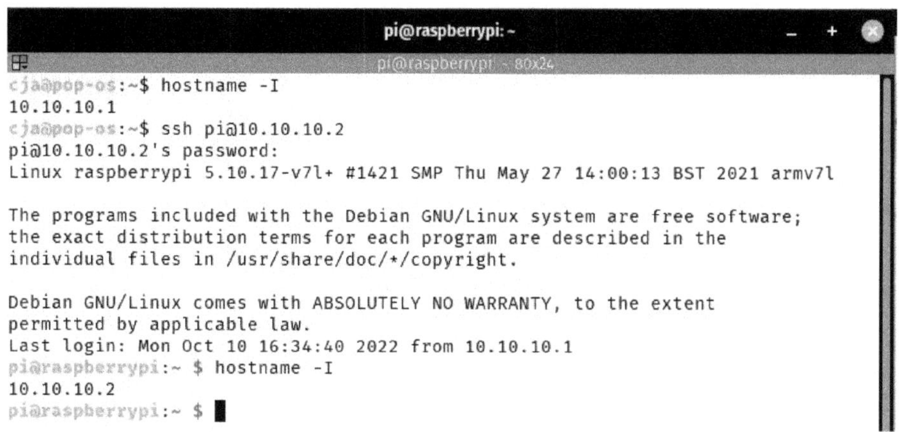

Now you can try any commands on your Pi through this Terminal remotely without having to access your Pi physically, via the connected monitor, keyboard and mouse. Try a few commands from Chapter V. Observe that the screenshot has a white background with a black font, I changed this so that the screenshot is clearly visible, in your case it will be a black backgroud with green/white font.

Also, *cja@pop-os:~$* is my computer with ip address 10.10.10.1, which is running a version of Ubuntu Linux and once the command is successful we see - *pi@raspberrypi:~ $* , this means we have logged into the Pi via SSH.

Once you are done with testing a few commands from Chapter V, to exit back to your computer command prompt, use the command exit
pi@raspberrypi:~ $ exit
logout
Connection to 10.10.10.2 closed.
cja@pop-os:~$

Note: For Microsoft Windows, if you are using the latest version of Windows 10 and higher, you will not need an extra tool like Putty, you can directly use the command prompt to SSH.

File Transfer

There are multiple ways to transfer files two and from your Pi to your laptop/computer -.

Using SCP (Secure Copy)

The fastest way to copy files to your Raspberry Pi is with SCP, which stands for "Secure Copy". SCP is based on the SSH protocol, so you'll need to enable SSH Pi before you use this method, this is described a couple of pages ago using the command *sudo raspi-config*

To transfer the file from your computer/laptop to the Pi, use the command

scp computerFile.txt pi@10.10.10.2:Downloads/

```
pi@raspberrypi: ~/Downloads
pi@raspberrypi: ~/Downloads 80x24
cja@pop-os:~/Documents$ cat computerFile.txt
File on my computer that needs to be tranfered
to the Pi.

cja@pop-os:~/Documents$ scp computerFile.txt pi@10.10.10.2:Downloads/
pi@10.10.10.2's password:
computerFile.txt                              100%   59     6.3KB/s   00:00
cja@pop-os:~/Documents$ ssh pi@10.10.10.2
pi@10.10.10.2's password:
Linux raspberrypi 5.10.17-v7l+ #1421 SMP Thu May 27 14:00:13 BST 2021 armv7l

The programs included with the Debian GNU/Linux system are free software;
the exact distribution terms for each program are described in the
individual files in /usr/share/doc/*/copyright.

Debian GNU/Linux comes with ABSOLUTELY NO WARRANTY, to the extent
permitted by applicable law.
Last login: Mon Oct 10 16:35:33 2022 from 10.10.10.1
pi@raspberrypi:~ $ cd Downloads
pi@raspberrypi:~/Downloads $ ls
computerFile.txt
pi@raspberrypi:~/Downloads $ 
```

This command will ask you for the password for the Pi. The computerFile.txt is transferred to the Downloads folder on the Pi in the home directory, that is /home/pi/Downloads.

To verify this, open another terminal/putty session, and SSH into the Pi and go to the Downloads folder to verify that the file was successfully transferred. If you remember from Chapter V, you will have to give the command "cd Downloads" followed by "ls".

For the vice-versa, that is to copy the file testFile.txt from your Pi to the current directory on your computer/laptop use the command -

scp pi@10.10.10.2:Downloads/testFile.txt .

Don't forget to first create the testFile.txt in the Download folder of your Pi, by using ssh, followed by "cd Downloads" followed by "nano testFile.txt". Once the command completes you should see the file on your computer/ laptop.

Using an SFTP (Secure File Transfer Protocol) client like FileZilla

You can transfer files to and from your Pi device by using a file-transfer protocol called SFTP. SFTP is a network protocol that provides secure file transfers over a network. This protocol can also be used to change, browse and edit files on your Raspberry Pi. Because SSH is used, all data transmitted over the network (including usernames and passwords) is encrypted and secure from eavesdropping.

To start, you need to install an SFTP client like FileZilla, this software is available for Microsoft Windows, Mac and Linux OS. Once you have the FileZilla window, type the IP address of your Pi, enter the username that is Pi and the password, enter port 22, and click Quickconnect to establish a remote connection.

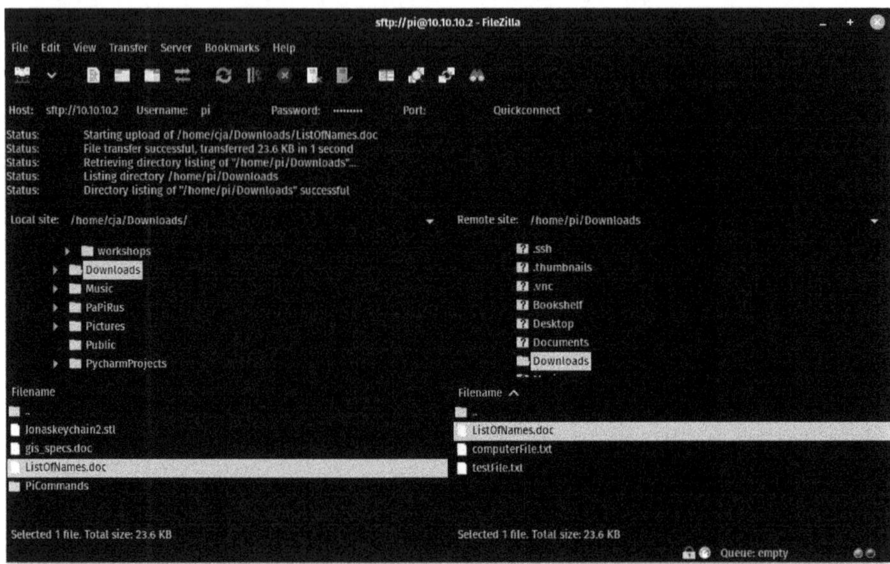

On the left, you will have a source repository which is your computer/ laptop and the destination server on the right which is your Pi. You can drag and drop files between the Pi and your computer/laptop. And vice-versa from your computer/laptop to the Pi.

At the start of each file transfer, you should see a report in the bottom transfer status window. Note that there are three tabs: Queued Files, Failed Transfers, and Successful Transfers. You can check that the file was successfully transferred by inspecting these three boxes.

Accessing the Pi Desktop Remotely

Consider a scenario where you are using the Pi in headless mode for a project, that is the Pi is not connected to a Monitor, Keyboard or Mouse. And you still want to use the Pi's PIXEL desktop, for this, you will have to use VNC

VNC is a graphical desktop sharing system that allows you to remotely control the desktop interface of one computer (running VNC Server) from another computer or mobile device (running VNC Viewer). VNC Viewer transmits the keyboard and either mouse or touch events to VNC Server, and receives updates to the screen in return. You will see the desktop of the

Pi inside a window on your computer. You'll be able to control it as though you were working on the Pi itself.

VNC Connect from RealVNC is included with the Raspberry Pi OS. It consists of both VNC Server, which allows you to control your Raspberry Pi remotely and VNC Viewer, which allows you to control desktop computers remotely from your Pi, should you wish.

To start you need to enable VNC using the raspi-config command and then go to the Interface section or use the Raspberry Pi configuration application in the Preference section of the application menu. In the interface tab, enable the VNC option.

pi@raspberrypi:~ $ sudo raspi-config

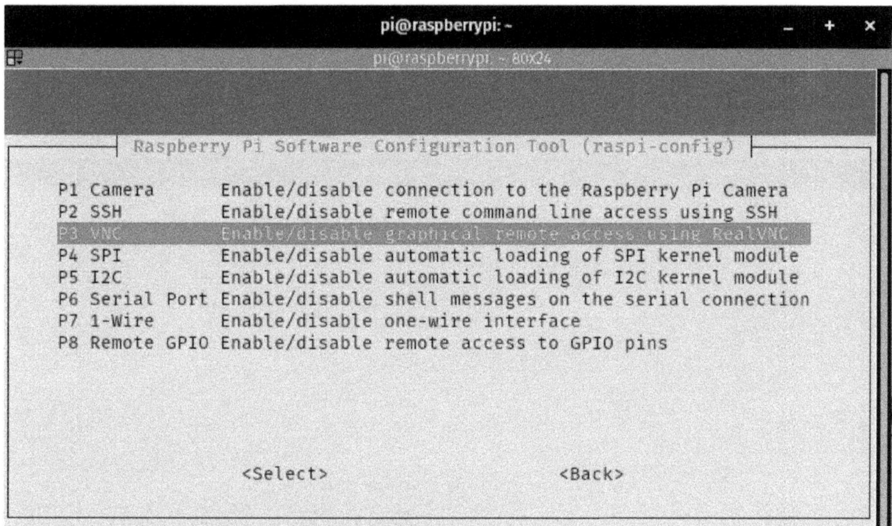

Now that you connect from your computer/laptop, you will need the VNC viewer application, and will have to download this from RealVNC.com website. You have an application for Microsoft Windows, macOS and Linux.

Once you have successfully installed the VNC viewer application, ssh into your Pi, run the vncserver command and make a note of the IP address and display number.

ssh pi@10.10.10.2

pi@raspberrypi:~ $ vncserver

You will see a long output, with the last few lines showing the VNC server catchphrase, signature and IP address:display number, as shown below.

Running applications in /etc/vnc/xstartup
VNC Server catchphrase: "Heart pupil ship. Heaven sweet Monaco."
signature: 9f-38-41-bc-e2-7b-d0-4a
Log file is /home/pi/.vnc/raspberrypi:1.log
New desktop is raspberrypi:1 (10.10.10.2:1)

Open the VNC viewer application on your computer/laptop and type in the Pi's IP address followed by the display number, like 10.10.10.2:1 and hit Enter. You are shown the catchphrase and Signature for validation and then you will be prompted to enter your username as Pi and the password. Once done you should see the VNC session on your computer/laptop.

Stopping the remote virtual desktop is also easy. Just use the command vncserver -kill :display number.

pi@raspberrypi:~ $ vncserver -kill :1

Other useful commands

wget

wget is a free utility that allows the downloading of files from the internet. It supports popular network protocols such as FTP, HTTP, and HTTPS. This command is handy when you are working on Pi projects and want to download a file from the internet quickly, the file could be anything: a jpg, a python code file, a Zip , a pdf, etc. You just need to URL the file.

pi@raspberrypi:~ $wget https://goanfpv.in/images/ShenDrone.jpg

Here we are downloading the header image (ShenDrone.jpg) from the website goanfpv.in.

Rsync

You can use rsync to synchronize folders between computers. You might want to transfer some files from your computer/ laptop to your Pi and for them to be kept up-to-date, or you might want the pictures taken by your Pi camera transferred to your computer automatically.

Using rsync over SSH allows you to transfer files to your computer/ laptop automatically.

On your computer/laptop, create a folder called camera.

Look up the Pi's IP address by running "hostname -I". In this example, the Raspberry Pi is creating a timelapse by capturing a photo every minute and saving the picture with a timestamp in the local folder camera on its SD card.

Now run the following command (substituting your own Raspberry Pi's IP address) -

rsync -avz -e ssh pi@10.10.10.2:camera/ camera/

This will copy all files from the Raspberry Pi's camera folder to your computer's/laptop's new camera folder.

Taking pictures and timelapse with the Pi camera/USB camera, will be discussed in detail in the next chapter - VIII.

CHAPTER VIII

Using the Pi Camera and USB webcam

Raspberry Pi currently sells two types of camera boards - a 8MP device and a 12MP High Quality (HQ) camera. The 8MP device is also available in NoIR form without an IR filter, idea for night vision. The original 5MP device is no longer available from Raspberry Pi. All Raspberry Pi cameras are capable of taking high-resolution photographs, along with full HD 1080p video, and can be fully controlled programmatically.

Connecting the Camera to the Pi

The flex cable inserts into the CSI connector on the Raspberry Pi, which is located between the Ethernet and micro HDMI ports. The cable must be inserted with the silver contacts facing the HDMI port. To open the connector, pull the tabs on the top of the connector upwards, then towards the Ethernet port. The flex cable should be inserted firmly into the connector, with care not to bend the flex at too acute an angle. To close the connector, push the top part of the connector towards the HDMI port and down, while holding the flex cable in place.

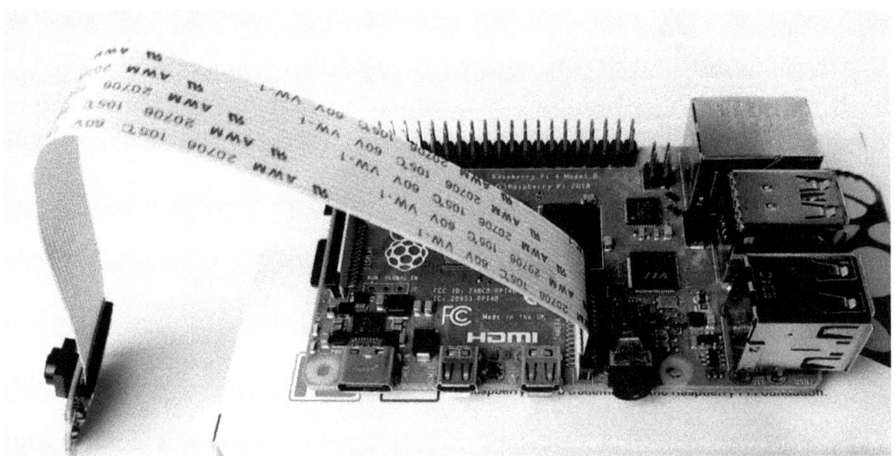

Enabling the Pi Camera in Raspberry Pi OS

To use the Pi camera you will have to first enable the Pi camera. You can use “sudo raspi-config”, followed by selecting the Interface option and selecting Camera, which will prompt with - “Would you like a Pi camera” choose “Yes”. Press Enter again at the confirmation box. This is ideal, if you are running your Pi headless. If not, you can also use the Raspberry Pi Configuration tool in the Preference section of the Application menu. And then click the Enable radio button.

pi@raspberrypi:~ $ sudo raspi-config

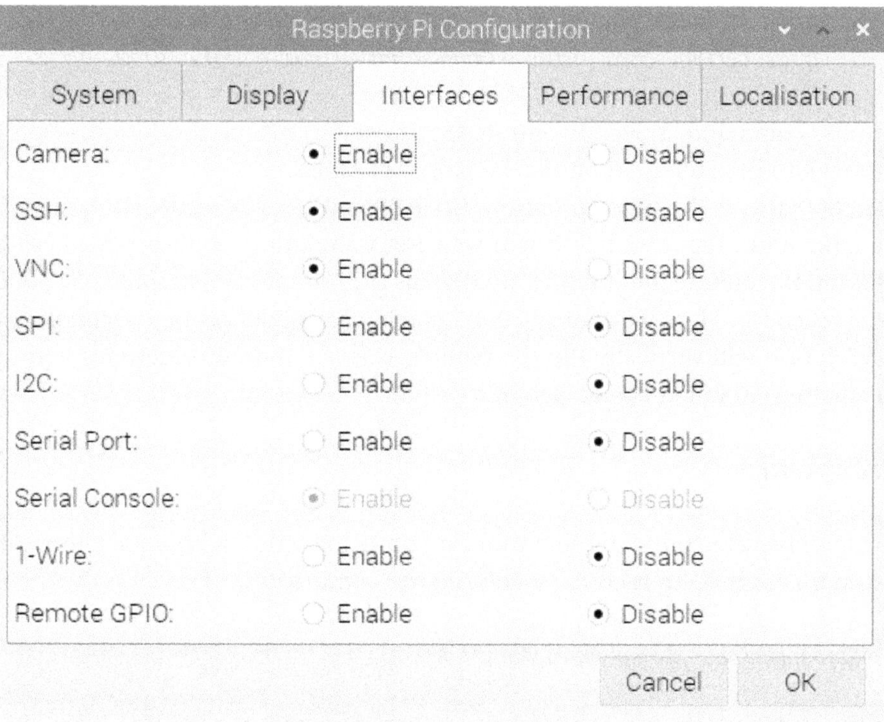

You will need to reboot after doing this. Once rebooted, start a terminal and try the command below to see if you are able to take a picture with the camera.

raspistill

raspistill is the command line tool for capturing still photographs with a Raspberry Pi camera module.

pi@raspberrypi:~ $raspistill -o image1.jpg

If everything is working correctly, the camera should start, a preview from the camera should appear on the display and, after a 5 second delay it should capture an image. Here the -o option is for the output file name. If you don't specify the full directory path the image will be saved to the current directory.
To capture an image at a different resolution use the command
pi@raspberrypi:~ $raspistill -o image2.jpg -w 640 -h 480 -t 2000 -vf

In the command above, -w 640 -h 480 is used to set the resolution, –w for the width in pixels, and –h for the height in pixels.
-t 2000, this is the timeout option. Basically, once you execute the raspistill command in the terminal, it will wait for x amount of milliseconds before taking the picture and exiting. By default the amount is 5 seconds, or 5000 milliseconds. Here we choose 2000, which means 2000ms or 2 seconds.
-vf option will vertically flip the picture, this is required sometimes if your camera is mounted upside down.

raspivid

raspivid is the command line tool for capturing video with a Raspberry Pi camera module. To record a video run the command -

pi@raspberrypi:~ $raspivid -o vid.h264

This will save a 5 second video file as vid.h264. To view the video use the VLC media player application. To specify the length of the video taken, use the -t flag with a number of milliseconds.

pi@raspberrypi:~ $raspivid -o video.h264 -t 20000

This will record 20 seconds of video.

Making a video

Once all of the images have been captured for your timelapse, they need to be strung together into one video file. To create the time-lapse video, use a utility called FFmpeg. FFmpeg is a free and open-source software project consisting of a suite of libraries and programs for handling video, audio, and other multimedia files and streams. At its core is the command-line ffmpeg tool itself, designed for processing of video and audio files.To start, download the FFmpeg package using -

pi@raspberrypi:~ $sudo apt install ffmpeg

This will take a few minutes depending on your internet speed. Once the package is successfully installed, create the final video using -

pi@raspberrypi:~ $ffmpeg -r 5 -i image%04d.jpg -c:v libx264 timelapseVideo.mp4

In the command above, the number after -r will determine how many frames are placed in each second of the video. Once the command completes , you can play the video file timelapseVideo.mp4 using the VLC player.

Before taking your Pi and Camera setup to the beach to make a timelapse of the sunset, refer to the last section of chapter IX which shows you how to automate the time lapse. So that you don't have to log into your Pi via SSH or carry a laptop, while you are enjoying the sunset on the beach.

Creating Timelapse

Timelapse refers to the process of capturing still images of a subject or scenery over a long period of time. By combining the images together, a video can be produced. Timelapse videos can be used for monitoring plant growth, watching the seasons change, capturing the sunset at the beach or even making a security camera keeping in mind the low storage capacity.

To create a timelapse video, you simply configure the Raspberry Pi to take a picture at a regular interval, such as once a minute, then use an application to stitch the pictures together into a video.

pi@raspberrypi:~ $raspistill -t 30000 --timelapse 2000 -o image%04d.jpg

The command above will produce a capture every two seconds (2000ms), over a total period of 30 seconds (30000ms), named image0001.jpg, image0002.jpg, and so on, through to image0015.jpg. The %04d indicates a four-digit number, with leading zeros added to make up the required number of digits.

USB Webcam

In most cases, in your projects, it is best to use a Raspberry Pi camera module. However, if you don't have a Pi camera handy, you can still create an awesome timelapse and other camera projects using your USB Webcam. USB Webcams generally have an inferior quality to the Pi camera, and cannot be controlled by the Pi camera commands - raspistill and raspivid. To control the USB Webcam, you will need a utility called fswebcam.

Taking pictures

To start install the fswebcam package using the Terminal application on the Pi, use the command

pi@raspberrypi:~ $sudo apt install fswebcam

Connect the USB webcam to one of the USB ports on the Pi. And to check if it is detected successfully by the Raspberry Pi OS use the command

pi@raspberrypi:~ $lsusb

```
pi@raspberrypi: ~
File  Edit  Tabs  Help
pi@raspberrypi:~ $ lsusb
Bus 002 Device 001: ID 1d6b:0003 Linux Foundation 3.0 root hub
Bus 001 Device 004: ID 046d:0825 Logitech, Inc. Webcam C270
Bus 001 Device 002: ID 2109:3431 VIA Labs, Inc. Hub
Bus 001 Device 001: ID 1d6b:0002 Linux Foundation 2.0 root hub
pi@raspberrypi:~ $
```

If you see a device that represents your USB webcam, like Logitech, Inc webcam C270. You can then run the command -

pi@raspberrypi:~ $fswebcam webcamImage.jpg

You can also specify the resolution of the image using the -r flag

pi@raspberrypi:~ $fswebcam -r 1280x720 webcamImage2.jpg

And to remove the banner from the image use the --no-banner flag

pi@raspberrypi:~ $fswebcam -r 1280x720 --no-banner image3.jpg

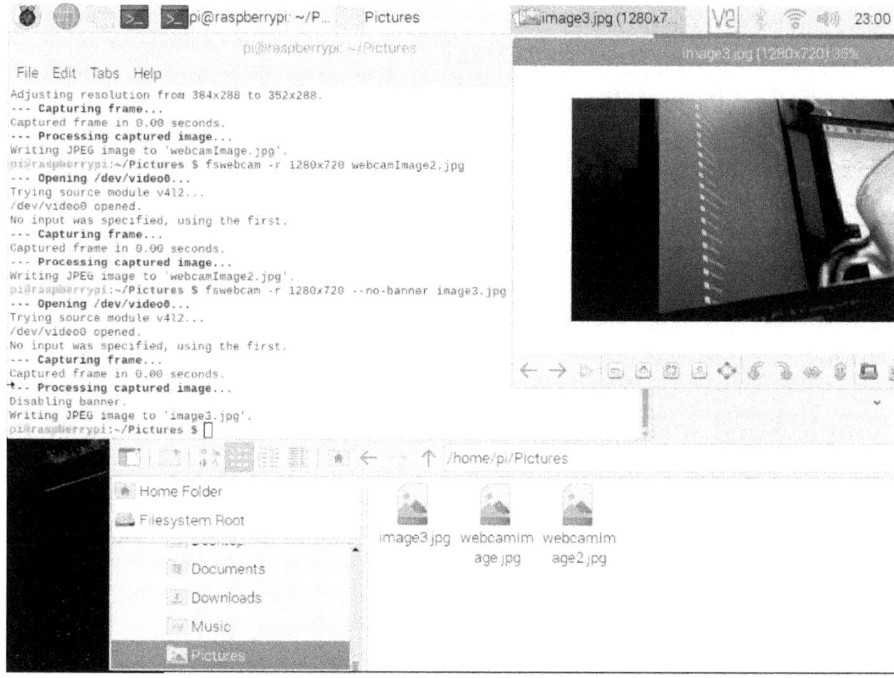

And just in case you are interested in finding the resolutions supported by the webcam use the command

pi@raspberrypi:~ $v4l2-ctl --list-formats-ext

CHAPTER IX

Shell Scripting and Automating Tasks on the Pi

A shell script is a command line program that contains a series of commands. An interpreter executes the commands contained in the script. In the case of shell scripts, the shell acts as the interpreter and executes the commands listed in the script one after the other.

The Raspberry Pi comes with the bash shell by default, so in this chapter, you will explore the usage of the bash shell in the Raspberry Pi. You can put anything you can execute at the Pi command line into a shell script. If you find yourself running a series of commands to accomplish a given task and will need to perform that task again in the future, you can and probably should create a shell script for that task.

Bash shell is the short form of the "Bourne Again Shell" which is the advanced form of the Bourne shell and is used in the UNIX operating systems, including the distributions of Linux like the Raspberry Pi Operating system that is based on Debian.

As part of shell scripting, you can type the different commands in the text file to run some particular tasks and then name the file with the extension of the "sh". This file will be executable and is known as the shell script.

Simple Shell script example

Here is a simple shell script. Use the nano editor in the Terminal application, type the two lines mentioned below, and name the script - script1.sh.

```
#!/bin/bash
echo "Scripting is fun!"
```

Before you try to execute the script, make sure that it is executable by using the chmod command, which was discussed in detail in chapter V

pi@raspberrypi:~ $ chmod 755 script1.sh

To execute the script, type the command below, and you should see the output of the echo command.

pi@raspberrypi:~ $ ./script1.sh
Scripting is fun!

You will notice that the first line of the script starts has #! followed by the path to the bash shell program, that is /bin/bash. The number "#" sign is very similar to the sharp sign used in music notation. And people refer to the exclamation mark as a "bang". So, "#!" can be called "sharp bang.", which gave rise to the term "Shebang" as a short form.

When a script's first line starts with a shebang, what follows is used as the interpreter for the commands listed in the script. When you execute a script that contains a shebang, what actually happens is that the interpreter is executed, and the path used to call the script is passed as an argument to the interpreter. You can check this by examining the process table using the ps command. To prove this, let's start by creating a shell script called sleeptest.sh. The contents of sleeptest.sh -

#!/bin/bash
sleep 120

Make the script executable using the chmod command.

pi@raspberrypi:~ $ chmod 755 sleeptest.sh

Execute the script in the background and take a look at the processes

pi@raspberrypi:~ $ ./sleeptest.sh &

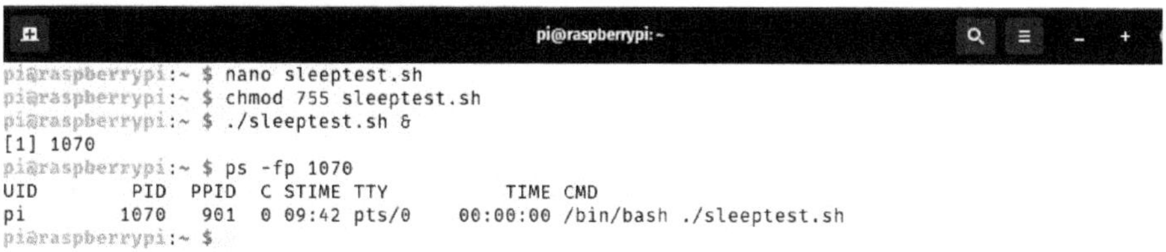

```
pi@raspberrypi:~
pi@raspberrypi:~ $ nano sleeptest.sh
pi@raspberrypi:~ $ chmod 755 sleeptest.sh
pi@raspberrypi:~ $ ./sleeptest.sh &
[1] 1070
pi@raspberrypi:~ $ ps -fp 1070
UID        PID  PPID  C STIME TTY          TIME CMD
pi        1070   901  0 09:42 pts/0    00:00:00 /bin/bash ./sleeptest.sh
pi@raspberrypi:~ $
```

If you do not supply a shebang and specify an interpreter on the first line of the script, the commands in the script will be executed using your current shell. Even though this can work just fine under many circumstances, it's best to be explicit and specify the exact interpreter to be used with the script,which in the case above is the bash shell.

Display text

Most of the shell commands tend to produce a specific output displayed on your console monitor where you are running the script. You may need to add text messages to help the script user know what will happen inside the script. You can do this by using the echo command. The echo command displays simple text strings.

pi@raspberrypi:~ $ echo I am learning shell scripting
I am learning shell scripting

The most remarkable thing is that you do not have to use quotes to enclose the string text, as with other programming languages. However, sometimes it becomes necessary to use quotes. Either you need single or double quotes to display the text strings.

pi@raspberrypi:~ $ echo "I am learning shell scripting."
I am learning shell scripting.

Using Variables

Every programming language has the concept of variables, which is a symbolic name for a chunk of memory to which we can assign values, read, and manipulate its contents.

```
#!/bin/sh
MY_MESSAGE="Hello Pi"
echo $MY_MESSAGE
```

This assigns the string "Hello Pi" to the variable MY_MESSAGE and then echoes out the variable's value. You will need quotes around the string Hello Pi. Whereas we could get away with echo Hello Pi, because echo will take any number of parameters, a variable can only hold one value. So a string with spaces must be quoted so that the shell knows to treat it all as one. The shell does not care about types of variables, and they may store strings, integers, real numbers or more.

Comments

Anything that follows the pound sign "#" is a comment. The only exception to this is the shebang (#!) on the first line. Comments are ignored by the interpreter and are usually helpful to someone reading, maintaining or enhancing your script in the future.

```
#!/bin/bash
sleep 10
#this is a comment line, and is ignored by the interpreter
echo "hello from the Raspberry Pi"
```

In the above example, since the pound sign starts at the beginning of a line the interpreter ignores the entire line. If a pound sign is encountered in the middle of a line, only the information to the right of the pound sign is ignored.

Getting User Input

Sometimes you may need to get user input in a shell script. If you want to accept standard input via the keyboard, use the read command. Standard input typically comes from a person typing at the keyboard, but it can also come from other sources, like the output of a command in a command line.

```
#!/bin/bash
read -p "enter name:" name
echo "you entered $name"
```

Just in case you want to hide the user input in a scenario where you are asking for the password, use read -s -p, using nano editor in the terminal application, type in text below, and save the file as userInput.sh

#!/bin/bash
read -p "enter user name:" user
read -s -p "enter password:" password
echo
echo "Your user name entered : $user"
echo "Your password: $password" # this is just for demo, for security, never reprint a password.

pi@raspberrypi:~ $ chmod 755 userInput.sh
pi@raspberrypi:~ $ ./userInput.sh

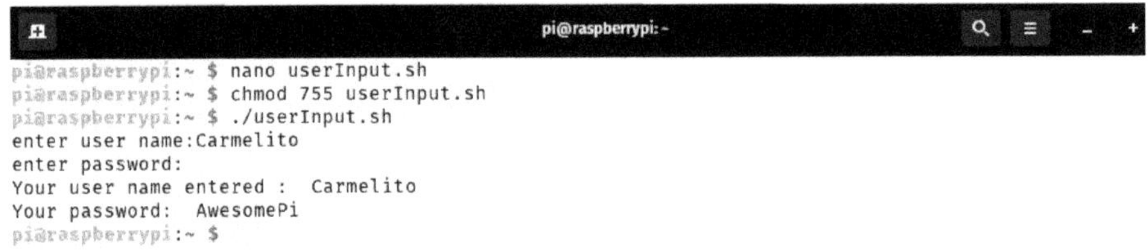

Conditional statements

Many Linux shell scripting programs require some logic flow control between different commands inside the script, which means that the shell tends to execute various commands. In addition, it keeps the ability to run different other commands that permit the script to loop through the commands based on the result of other commands. We refer to them as structured commands, also known as conditional statements.

The conditional statement is used in any programming language to perform decision-making tasks. This statement is also used in bash to perform automated tasks like other programming languages, but bash syntax is slightly different. Two types of conditional statements can be used in bash. These are 'If' and 'case' statements.

if-else Statement

One of the most important parts of conditional programming is the if-else statements. An if-else statement allows you to execute iterative conditional statements in your code. The if-else block is one, if not the most essential, part of conditional programming. By regulating the execution of specific statements you not only make your code more efficient but also frees up precious time that the processor might have wasted executing statements which are unnecessary for a specific case.

We use if-else in shell scripts when we wish to evaluate a condition, then decide to execute one set between two or more sets of statements using the result.

```
if condition
then
statement1
else
statement2
fi
```

Here we have four keywords: if, then, else and fi.

- The keyword if is followed by a condition.
- This condition is evaluated to decide which statement will be executed by the processor.
- If the condition evaluates to TRUE, the processor will execute the statement(s) followed by the keyword then. In the syntax, it is mentioned as statement1.
- In a case where the condition evaluates to FALSE, the processor will execute the statement(s) followed by the keyword else. This is denoted as statement2 in the function syntax.

An important thing to keep in mind is that, like C programming, shell scripting is case-sensitive. Hence, you need to be careful while using the keywords in your code.

When trying to understand the working of a function like if-else in a shell script, it is good to start things simple. Here, we initialize two variables m and n, then use the if-else function to check if the two variables are equal. The bash script should look as follows -

```
#!/bin/bash
m=1
n=2
if [ $n -eq $m ]
then
echo "Both variables are the same"
else
echo "Both variables are different"
fi
```

Output of running the above shell script is -
Both variables are different

Like the -eq operator between the two variables in the if condition, here is the list of the other operators -

- && Logical AND
- $0 Argument 0 i.e. the command that's used to run the script
- $1 First argument (change number to access further arguments)
- -eq Equality check
- -ne Inequality check
- -lt Less Than
- -le Less Than or Equal
- -gt Greater Than
- -ge Greater Than or Equal

Here is another example for password checking

```
#!/bin/bash
read -p "Enter password : " passwd
if [ $passwd = "password" ]
then
echo "The password is correct."
else
echo "The password is incorrect, try again."
fi
```

In this example, we will use if-else in a shell script to make the interface for a password prompt. To do this, we will ask the user to enter the password and store it in the variable pass. If it matches the pre-defined password, which is 'password' in this example, the user will get the output as -"The password is correct". Else, the shell script will tell the user that the password was incorrect and ask them to try again.

Case Statement

Sometimes, we may wish to take different paths based on a variable matching a series of patterns. We could use a series of if and elif statements, but that would soon grow and be unmanageable. Fortunately, there is a case statement which can make things cleaner.

The basic syntax of the case...esac statement is to give an expression to evaluate and to execute several different statements based on the value of the expression. The interpreter checks each case against the value of the expression until a match is found. If nothing matches, a default condition will be used. Here is a simple example -

```
#!/bin/bash
#get the name of the planet from the user
read -p "Enter name of the planet: " planet
case "$planet" in
"Mercury") echo "The smallest planet in our solar system."
;;
"Venus") echo "Spins slowly in the opposite direction"
;;
"Earth") echo "Our home planet"
;;
"Mars") echo "Dusty, Cold, with a very thin atmosphere."
;;
*) echo "No planet with the name $planet" #default condition if no match is
found.
;;
esac
```

Loops

Loops allow us to take a series of commands and keep re-running them until a particular situation is reached. They are useful for automating repetitive tasks. If we want to repeat a task twenty times, we don't want to have to type in the code twenty times, with maybe a slight change each time. As a result, we have for and while loops -

For Loops

Using the for loop in shell scripts is reasonably straightforward, and you can manipulate the structure to achieve different goals. For iterates over a list. As long as it finds an item in the list, for loop continues to iterate over the list and stops iteration once it reaches the end of the list.

```
for var in list
do
commands
done
```

Here is an example of a for loop that prints the current value of i, as the loop goes through each iteration.

```
#!/bin/bash
for i in 1 2 3
do
echo "Current Value # $i"
done
```

i = variable name to store the iterated values
1 2 3 = number of times the for loop in shell script iterates
do = command to perform a certain set of actions
echo = print the results defined alongside
done = end of the loop

While Loop

The while loop allows for repetitive execution of a list of commands, as long as the condition is true. Once the condition is false, while loop stops execution.

```
    while condition
do
commands
done
```

Here is an example of a basic while loop

```
#!/bin/bash
i=1
while [ $i -le 5 ]
do
echo "$i"
((i++)) ## increments i by one each iteration
done
```

Until Loop

The until loop is almost equal to the while loop, except that the code is executed while the condition evaluates to false.

```
until condition
do
command
done
```

Here is an example of a basic until loop. Observe the condition, it is exactly opposite of the while loop that is i is greater than or equal to 5

```
#!/bin/bash
i=1
until [ $i -gt 5 ]
do
echo $i ## returns 1 2 3 4 5
((i++))
done
```

Exit Status and Return codes

Every time a command is executed it returns an exit status. The exit status, which is sometimes called a return code or exit code, is an integer ranging from 0 to 255. By convention, commands that execute successfully return a 0 exit status. If some sort of error is encountered, then a non-zero exit status is returned.

These return codes can be used in your script for error checking. It can be a simple test, like checking for a zero return code, or it could be more complex, like checking for a specific error code.

To find out what the various exit statuses mean, you have to consult the documentation for the given command or look at its source code. You can use the man and info commands to read the documentation for most commands on your system. For example, the grep man page, it explains grep will exit with a status of 0 if the search pattern is found and 1 if it is not.

The special variable $? Contains the return code of the previously executed command. In this shell script snippet, the ls command is called with a path to a file that doesn't exist.

```
#!/bin/bash
ls /not/here
echo "$?"
```

Output of the script -

```
ls: cannot access '/not/here ': No such file or directory
2
```

In the script immediately after the ls command is executed, the return code of that command is displayed on the screen using echo $?. This will display a 2 on the screen. Remember that non-zero exit codes indicate some sort of error. Had the file /not/here existed, and if ls could display information about that file successfully, the exit status would have been 0.

You can use the exit status of a command to make a decision or perform a different action based on the exit status. In this example shell script snippet, we use the ping command to test our network connectivity to www.google.com. The -c option for the ping command simply tells ping to send just one packet.

```
#!/bin/bash
HOST="google.com"
```

```
ping -c 1 $HOST
if [ "$?" -eq "0" ]
then
echo "$HOST reachable."
else
echo "$HOST not reachable."
fi
```

```
pi@raspberrypi: ~
pi@raspberrypi:~ $ nano pingWebsite.sh
pi@raspberrypi:~ $ chmod 755 pingWebsite.sh
pi@raspberrypi:~ $ ./pingWebsite.sh
PING google.com (172.217.27.206) 56(84) bytes of data.
64 bytes from bom07s15-in-f14.1e100.net (172.217.27.206): icmp_seq=1 ttl=52 time=61.2 ms

--- google.com ping statistics ---
1 packets transmitted, 1 received, 0% packet loss, time 0ms
rtt min/avg/max/mdev = 61.211/61.211/61.211/0.000 ms
google.com reachable.
pi@raspberrypi:~ $
```

After the ping command is executed, the script checks the exit status. If the exit status is equal to 0, then we echo to the screen that google.com is reachable. If the exit status is NOT equal to 0 we echo to the screen that google.com is not reachable.

Shell scripting is a vast topic, the above serves as an introduction to shell scripting, which will enable you to understand and create simple scripts to automate multiple commands or tasks on your Raspberry Pi.

Running your program automatically

When running a Linux system, it is helpful to run tasks at a certain time or regularly. This can be useful for regular backups, performing routine checks on the system or running your own programs automatically. Linux is a relatively complex operating system, and as such, there are often multiple ways to achieve the same thing. To get a program to run on boot, there are multiple ways, but we will concentrate on the two popular ones being used today - Crontab and systemd.

crontab

Cron is a scheduler that can run commands at regular intervals. It's often referred to as crontab which is the name of the configuration file. Crontab stands for "cron table, " because it uses the job scheduler cron to execute tasks. Cron itself is named after "chronos", the Greek word for time.

To edit crontab entries, use crontab -e.

pi@raspberrypi:~ $ sudo crontab -e

Here is an output of an empty crontab file

 # For more information see the manual pages of crontab(5) and cron(8)

#

 # m h dom mon dow command

Each line reflects a single entry which has 5 time/date fields to specify when the commands are run followed by the command to execute

m - Minutes - 0 to 59

h - Hours - 0 to 23

dom - Days of Month - 1 to 31

mon - Month - 1 to 12 or JAN-DEC

dow - Day of week - 1 to 7 or MON-SUN (or 0 can be used for Sunday if preferred)

The fields can have a single value, comma separated values, range of values or an asterisk (*) for any value. Now lets looks at some examples -

* * * * * rm /home/someuser/tmp/*

The above entry if added to the crontab file will run every minute to delete all the files created in the tmp directory. The asterix (*) means all the possible units, that is every minute of every hour throughout the year. Ideally, you may not have a requirement to schedule a job every minute, so let's have it set for a particular time

30 16 * * * rm /home/someuser/tmp/*

In this example, the files in the tmp directory will be deleted at 16:30, that is 4:30 PM in the evening, just as you are about to finish your day's work.

0 0 11,18 * * * /home/pi/scripts/backup

In case you have a backup script and would like to backup, your work every day at 11:00 AM and 6:00 PM. The comma-separated value in a field specifies that the command needs to be executed at all the mentioned times.

*/15 * * * * /home/pi/scripts/networkStatus

This crontab entry will executes the script to check the network status every 15 minutes throughout the year.

Automating taking a timelapse

In chapter VIII, we learnt about the commands to create a time lapse. And if you want to take your project on the road, you must automate the timelapse. To start, create a shell script, which contains the raspistill command to take pictures, using the nano editor.

pi@raspberrypi:~ $ nano timelapse.sh

And then add the following text to the file

```
#!/bin/bash
DATE=$(date +"%Y-%m-%d_%H%M")
raspistill -o /home/pi/timelapse/image$DATE.jpg
```

If you observe in the raspistill command you will need to create a folder called timelapse, use the command

pi@raspberrypi:~ $mkdir timelapse

To make the shell script timelapse.sh executable use the chmod command

pi@raspberrypi:~ $ sudo chmod +x timelapse.sh

The next step to scheduling the timelapse to go off every minute, for this you will need to update the crontab *pi@raspberrypi:~ $ sudo crontab -e*

Add the entry below to the last line of the file

* * * * * /home/pi/*timelapse.sh* 2>&1

Once done, exit and save by pressing CTRL + X, then Y. You are done setting up the Raspberry Pi camera and the cron job, you can just disconnect and place the Pi and camera setup anywhere you would like. You don't need to have a screen connected to the Pi for it to work.

This method just saves the pictures directly to the Pi's SD card, and you can set it up to save to a USB stick, network drive and other places to store data.

Also, once you're done with your time lapse pictures, you must be anxious to share them on your social media platforms. For this, you can create a GIF using software like imagemagick. To install imagemagick use

pi@raspberrypi:~ $sudo apt-get install imagemagick

Once done, use the convert command, which is ImageMagick command line processing tool, to create a gif file by combining all the images.

pi@raspberrypi:~ $convert -delay 10 -loop 0 image.jpg animation.gif*

The -delay option sets the amount of time in 100ths of a second between frames. The -loop option sets the number of times the GIF will loop, here the 0 tells it to loop forever.

Systemd

Systemd is a new and popular way to automatically start programs in Linux. Systemd software manages the initialization of the system during system startup. Systemd is the one that starts all the key processes to get your Linux system properly running. This includes for example the mounting of the file systems, setting up networking and getting the display manager up-and-running. Besides managing the system initialization, Systemd also provides a services manager that assists with keeping your Linux system running.

Systemd can be quite complicated, and the steps below cover the basics to get you started running your programs on boot-

Creating a Unit File

If you want systemd to run a script at system startup on your Raspberry Pi, you need to first create a unit file using the format below

pi@raspberrypi:~ $ sudo nano /etc/systemd/system/systemInfo.service

Add the following lines once the nano editor opens

```
[Unit]
Description=Systemd service to log system info

[Service]
ExecStart=/home/pi/systemInfoScript.sh

[Install]
WantedBy=default.target
```

The Unit section at a minimum should contain a Description directive. It can contain other directives such as other Systemd units that it depends on. Systemd will start the dependent units automatically in parallel. The before/after directives could further influence the starting order if parallel activation is not desired. The example above is a simple service, which means this service does not depend on any other units and therefore only contains Description.

The second part of the unit file contains the Service section. In this case you only need to inform Systemd of the script/program you want it to start, with the help of the ExecStart directive. Usually, you would also include a Type directive here. Our service type is simple, which is the default service type if the Service section contains the ExecStart directive. For this reason the Type directive is not added. There are many more directives available for the Service section. For example the ExecStartPre/

ExecStartPost directives that allow you to specify a script/program that should be executed before or after the one specified with ExecStart. Other commonly used directives are Restart and RestartSec. These allow you specify conditions under which the script/program should be automatically restarted.

The last section is the install section and informs Systemd at which moment during the boot process the service should be started. During the boot process, Systemd boots your system step-by-step. Each step is a so-called target that Systemd attempts to reach. By specifying a specific target in the WantedBy directive, you can latch the service on to that target. This allows you to essentially control when Systemd starts your service. In our case we latch on to the default.target. On any Linux system with Systemd, it means the last target during the boot process. If you are curious about the available targets you can run the command (systemctl list-units --type=target) in the terminal.

Also create the shell script systemInfoScript.sh using nano editor, using the command

```
pi@raspberrypi:~ $ nano /home/pi/systemInfoScript.sh
```

And type in the following, once the nano editor opens

```
#!/bin/bash
# variable for log file location, as the input.
LOG_FILE="$1"
# Set a default log file location if the parameter is not specified.
if [ -z "$LOG_FILE" ]
then
LOG_FILE="/var/log/testSystemInfoLog.txt"
fi

# Append information to the log file.
echo "----------------------------------------" >> "$LOG_FILE"
echo "System date and time: $(date '+%d/%m/%Y %H:%M:%S')" >>
"$LOG_FILE"
echo "Kernel info: $(uname -rmv)" >> "$LOG_FILE"
echo "ip address: $(hostname -I)" >> "$LOG_FILE"
```

echo "CPU temperature: $(vcgencmd measure_temp)" >> "$LOG_FILE"

Enable the Service

Although you have stored the service file in the correct location, that is /etc/systemd/system/, the Raspberry Pi operating system will not run this script upon startup. For this to work we still need to enable it with Systemd. To enable the service with Systemd, use the command -

pi@raspberrypi:~ $sudo systemctl enable systemInfo.service

Now to test the service, reboot your Pi using the sudo reboot command. And once the Pi has booted up, check the testSystemInfoLog.txt file, using the command.

pi@raspberrypi:~ $ cat /var/log/testSystemInfoLog.txt

Since not all services will end up creating a file, another way to check is to check on the status using the command

pi@raspberrypi:~ $ systemctl status systemInfo.service

At any point if you need to disable the newly created service use the command

pi@raspberrypi:~ $ sudo systemctl disable systemInfo.service

Today almost all Linux distributions include Systemd. Which means your newly gained skill set of shell scripting and automation on the Raspberry Pi, will be handy on other Linux distributions as well.

CHAPTER X

Troubleshooting Common Issues

When using the Raspberry Pi device, the user can face many issues, which will produce hurdles in completing the project. This Chapter will address some common issues which you'll mostly face while using Raspberry Pi .

Red Power LED Blinking

If you notice a red blinking light on your Raspberry Pi, the chances are high that you have a power supply issue. If the power supply is dropping out and supplying less than the required power current for the model you are using, it will cause the red blinking.

Solution
To resolve this issue, you can use the recommended/official power supply created for the Pi.

Coloured Splash Screen

A coloured splash screen on the Raspberry Pi displays after you load the Raspberry Pi's GPU firmware (start.efl). However, when the splash screen displays, the Linux console automatically replaces it seconds later, which helps to troubleshoot and disable features that are causing problems. The primary cause of this issue is an issue of a corrupted kernel.img that renders the device unable to complete the boot process.

Solution
You can fix this problem by replacing the current kernel image with a compatible kernel image. This is an advanced topic, the easiest way would be to re-flash your SD card with the latest image of the Raspberry Pi OS.

Green LED blinking sequence issues

On most occasions, the Raspberry Pi LED will start to blink green in particular patterns. It is essential to note the pattern so that you can determine the cause of the problem.

- 1 Flash: This problem is a result of SD card issues and a failed boot device. It can, however, be a result of software issues, and it is a good idea to flash the Raspberry Pi with the latest software for the corresponding model.
- 2 Flashes: Two flashes are also a result of SD card read problems. You can solve this problem by formatting the SD card and reinstalling the OS.
- 3 Flashes: Indicates a start.elf is not found issue.
- 4 Flashes: Indicates a start.elf not launched issue.
- 7 Flashes: Indicates a kernel image file not found.
- 8 Flashes: SDRAM not recognised. Install a new bootcode.in/start.elf firmware.

Rebooting after some interval

Another common issue that Raspberry users face is rebooting the device after some time. You may lose your data if your device keeps on rebooting.

Solution

This unexpected rebooting of the Raspberry Pi is due to the power issue, and the Raspberry Pi board needs 5 Volts. If it is getting power lower than 5 Volts, it will reboot repeatedly and may not work at all. Ensure the data cable attached to the board is of good quality and provides the necessary power to the Raspberry Pi board.

USB device connected not working

Described below are scenarios where USB devices connected to the Raspberry Pi, are either not recognised by the Pi or do not work correctly.

Solution

There are multiple reasons that could cause this issue -

- The Raspberry Pi is probably not getting enough power and is thus unable to power the USB device. So ensure your Pi is properly powered.

- Connect your device to the Pi before turning it on. While this is a rare problem, for USB devices like your Keyboard and Mouse, the Pi might need to do some initialisation, especially if you are connecting it to the Pi for the first time. Here you can try the lsusb command to check if the USB device is detected. Like the screenshot below has detected the receiver of my Logitech B170 wireless mouse, as the second entry.

```
pi@raspberrypi: ~
pi@raspberrypi:~ $ lsusb
Bus 002 Device 001: ID 1d6b:0003 Linux Foundation 3.0 root hub
Bus 001 Device 004: ID 046d:c534 Logitech, Inc. Unifying Receiver
Bus 001 Device 002: ID 2109:3431 VIA Labs, Inc. Hub
Bus 001 Device 001: ID 1d6b:0002 Linux Foundation 2.0 root hub
```

- Potential driver issues.- To ensure the USB device is compatible with the Linux based operating system, check the Elinux.org website, which has a list of USB devices that are compatible with the Raspberry Pi. The list is quite well ordered and it should help you determine if your device is compatible or not.
- The USB device could be faulty. Test it with your computer/laptop to be sure it is working correctly.

Keyboard Character Displays wrong character

When the key displayed on the screen is different from the one pressed on the keyboard, especially the # key. This error occurs as a result of the default UK keyboard configuration, which you have not changed as part of the installation process.

Solution

To fix this, you will need to change the configuration to that of your own keyboard or language. This can be done by going to the raspi-config menu via command line or Raspberry Pi configuration application in the Preference section of the application menu. Go to the Internationalization menu, select the keyboard setup menu and scroll down to select the keyboard layout that matches the country of origin/language of your keyboard.

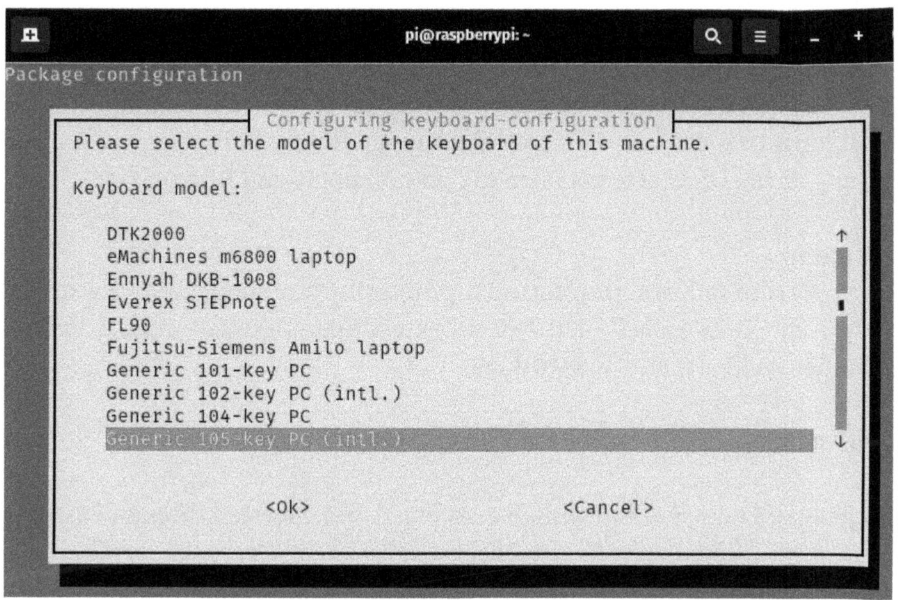

Sound does not work with an HDMI monitor

This is caused by some computer monitors which select DVI mode even if an HDMI cable is connected.

Solution

For this, you will have to update the config.txt file to force the OS to select HDMI mode. Using the nano editor update the /boot/config.txt.

hdmi_drive=2

And to run a quick test, play a .wav file, and double check your volume controls on the monitor.

pi@raspberrypi:~ $ aplay /usr/share/sounds/alsa/Front_Center.wav

Connected WiFi network drops intermittently

90% of all network problems related to connection problems are related to the power supply.The power supply is too weak or unsuitable for operation on Raspberry Pi with heavily fluctuating power consumption from additional USB devices. This can also happen if your Pi is using too long or an unsuitable USB cable between the power supply and Raspberry Pi.

Solution
For sporadic failures and network problems, you should first swap the power supply especially if the network configuration has worked before, and then suddenly stopped working.

Not able to SSH into the Pi or access VNC

Raspberry Pi devices can easily be accessed and operated through SSH, but many users, due to several reasons, are not able to access the Raspberry Pi over SSH. One of the most common reason is that you have forgotten the IP address of the Pi that is headless. Or you have not enabled the SSH and VNC in raspi-config.

Solution
Double check if you have enabled SSH and VNC in raspi-config or in the Raspberry Pi configuration application under the Preference section of the Application menu.

If you have forgotten your IP address, you can use a utility like nmap on your computer/laptop. You can use nmap to scan your local network to find all devices that are connected. To do this you have to find the IP address of your local computer, for -

- macOS - On a Mac, open the Network Utility (cmd + space, then search for Network Utility).
- Windows- On Windows, open the Network and Sharing Center (Control Panel > Network and Sharing).
- And in Linux - type hostname -I in the Terminal application.

Mostly, your IP address will likely be something like: 192.168.1.6 , so other devices on the same network are going to have addresses that share the first three octets: 192.168.1. The notation to describe the entire range of IP addresses between 192.168.1.0 and 192.168.1.255 is 192.168.1.0/24. You are now ready to use the nmap command on your laptop/computer -

nmap -sn 192.168.1.0/24

You'll notice here that a few devices are returned, but after a quick scan you'll notice a your Raspberry Pi connected to the network. From here you can discover the IP address of your Pi.

Troubleshooting Pi Camera issue

If your Pi reboots as soon as you run the commands, your power supply is insufficient for running your Pi plus the camera module (and whatever other peripherals you have attached).

Pi Camera not detected - double check the connection of the ribbon cable to the camera and CSI connector, this can become loose over a period of time, especially if you travel with the Pi a lot. Using a fingernail, flip up the connector on the PCB, then reconnect it with gentle pressure.
If something else happens, read the error message displayed and try any recommendations suggested by the error messages -

- Error : raspistill/raspivid command not found. This probably means your update/upgrade commands failed in some way. Try the commands again, and ensure you are connected to the internet.
- Error : ENOMEM. The Camera Module is not starting up. Check all connections again.
- Error : ENOSPC. The Camera Module is probably running out of GPU memory. Check config.txt in the /boot/ folder. The gpu_mem option should be at least 128. Alternatively, use the Memory Split option in the Advanced section of raspi-config to set this.

…nonths, you may observe the picture captured with a camera … black. This issue occurs due to the old versions of packages … sing the Raspberry Pi, make sure all the packages installed on the Raspberry Pi are up-to-date. To resolve this issue, run commands to upgrade the packages on the Raspberry Pi OS using -

pi@raspberrypi:~ $ sudo apt update && sudo apt full-upgrade -y

Using dmesg command for debugging

dmesg is a display message command, that display kernel-related messages on linux operating systems. The output contains messages produced by the device drivers. The Linux kernel is the core of the operating system that controls access to the system resources, such as central processing unit, Input/Output devices, physical memory, and file systems. The kernel writes several messages to the kernel ring buffer during the boot process and when the system is running.

dmesg is used to examine or control the kernel ring buffer. It is really useful for examining kernel boot messages and debugging hardware related issues. Since Pi is a non-root user you will have to use sudo to run the dmesg command.

pi@raspberrypi:~ $ sudo dmesg

To monitor real-time logs --follow option is used with dmesg, and it displays the recent messages at the bottom of the terminal

pi@raspberrypi:~ $ sudo dmesg --follow

If you find the dmesg output to be too large you can use the tail option with the pipe operator, this is something we covered in Chapter V.

pi@raspberrypi:~ $ sudo dmesg | tail -10

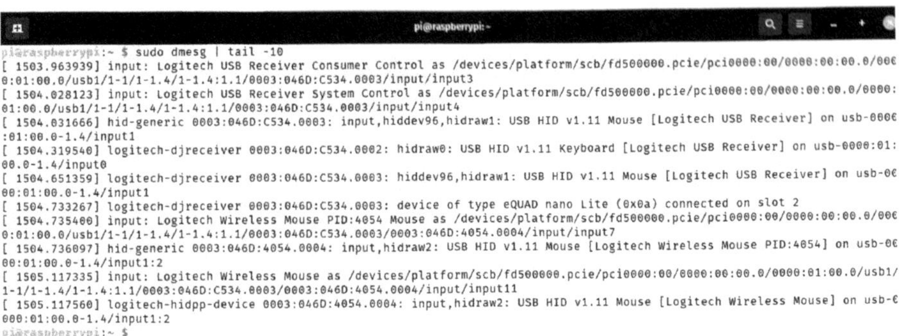

In case, you are debugging a specific issue with respect to a USB device you just connected to the Pi, you can use grep with the -i option to perform a string pattern search for USB.

pi@raspberrypi:~ $ sudo dmesg | grep -i usb

The message in dmesg has a level assigned to each message logged to the kernel ring buffer. The level represents the significance of the information in the communication. The levels are as follows -

- emerg: The system is unusable.
- alert: Action must be taken immediately.
- crit: Critical conditions.
- err: Error conditions.
- warn: Warning conditions.
- notice: Normal but significant condition.
- info: Informational.
- debug: Debug-level messages.

To extract messages linked to a specific level use the -l option. For example, if you are looking for errors and warning messages to display use

pi@raspberrypi:~ $ sudo dmesg --level=err,warn

```
pi@raspberrypi:~
pi@raspberrypi:~ $ sudo dmesg --level=err,warn
[    0.000000] Kernel parameter elevator= does not have any effect anymore.
               Please use sysfs to set IO scheduler for individual devices.
[    0.151567] usb_phy_generic phy: supply vcc not found, using dummy regulator
[    1.536139] mmc1: queuing unknown CIS tuple 0x80 (2 bytes)
[    1.537840] mmc1: queuing unknown CIS tuple 0x80 (3 bytes)
[    1.539542] mmc1: queuing unknown CIS tuple 0x80 (3 bytes)
[    1.542584] mmc1: queuing unknown CIS tuple 0x80 (7 bytes)
[    1.544321] mmc1: queuing unknown CIS tuple 0x80 (3 bytes)
[    4.827848] vc_sm_cma: module is from the staging directory, the quality is unknown, you have been warned.
[    4.831363] vc_sm_cma: module is from the staging directory, the quality is unknown, you have been warned.
[    4.840329] snd_bcm2835: module is from the staging directory, the quality is unknown, you have been warned.
[    4.842261] bcm2835_mmal_vchiq: module is from the staging directory, the quality is unknown, you have been warned.
[    4.843484] bcm2835_mmal_vchiq: module is from the staging directory, the quality is unknown, you have been warned.
[    4.844580] bcm2835_mmal_vchiq: module is from the staging directory, the quality is unknown, you have been warned.
[    4.849782] bcm2835_v4l2: module is from the staging directory, the quality is unknown, you have been warned.
[    4.857554] bcm2835_isp: module is from the staging directory, the quality is unknown, you have been warned.
[    4.865537] bcm2835_codec: module is from the staging directory, the quality is unknown, you have been warned.
[    5.326899] [drm] No displays found. Consider forcing hotplug if HDMI is attached
[    5.468537] brcmfmac: brcmf_fw_alloc_request: using brcm/brcmfmac43455-sdio for chip BCM4345/6
[    5.490446] brcmfmac mmc1:0001:1: Direct firmware load for brcm/brcmfmac43455-sdio.raspberrypi,4-model-b.txt failed with err
or -2
[    5.729681] brcmfmac: brcmf_fw_alloc_request: using brcm/brcmfmac43455-sdio for chip BCM4345/6
[    5.743334] brcmfmac: brcmf_c_preinit_dcmds: Firmware: BCM4345/6 wl0: Jan  4 2021 19:56:29 version 7.45.229 (617f1f5 CY) FWI
D 01-2dbd9d2e
[    8.339069] brcmfmac: brcmf_cfg80211_set_power_mgmt: power save enabled
pi@raspberrypi:~ $
```

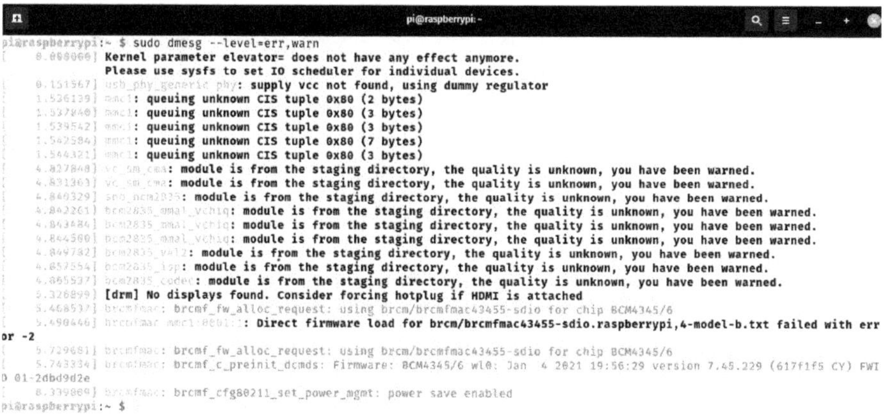

Using htop or Task Manager to check on Pi's performance

Both the task manager and htop are powerful utilities that allow you to interactively monitor your Pi's vital resources and processes in real-time.

htop also supports mouse operations, uses colors in its outputs and gives visual indications about processor, memory and swap usage. The top-left panel in the screen, corresponds to CPU and Memory usage.The count 1-4, represents the cores/CPUs of the system. The bar describes the amount and type of processes using each core. The value against the bar denotes the percentage each core is being consumed.

pi@raspberrypi:~ $htop

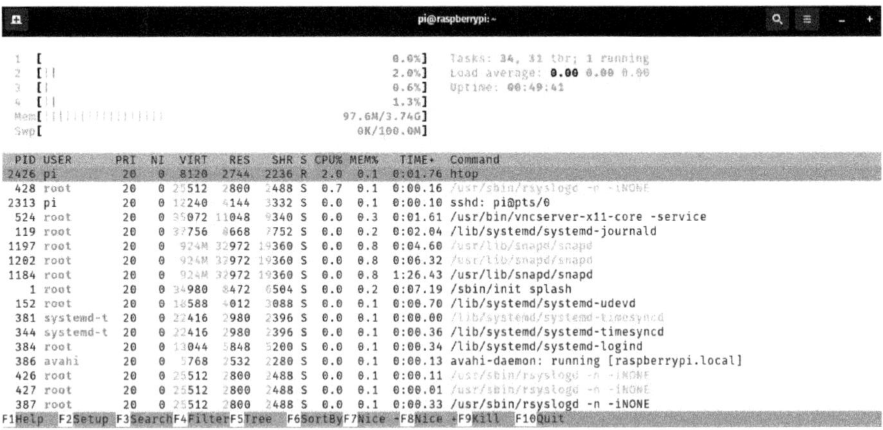

Color coding for CPU [1,2,3,4]- as it is quite visible to the user, there are multiple colors used to describe the bar. each color has a specific meaning

- Green - Amount of CPU consumed by the user's processes.
- Red - Amount of CPU used by system processes.
- Grey - Amount of CPU used for Input/Output based processes

Color coding for Memory [Mem] - on the similar lines for memory, the meaning of each color is

- Green - Percentage of RAM being used for running processes in the system.
- Blue - Percentage of RAM being consumed by buffer pages.

Mostly, your IP address will likely be something like: 192.168.1.6 , so other devices on the same network are going to have addresses that share the first three octets: 192.168.1. The notation to describe the entire range of IP addresses between 192.168.1.0 and 192.168.1.255 is 192.168.1.0/24. You are now ready to use the nmap command on your laptop/computer -

nmap -sn 192.168.1.0/24

You'll notice here that a few devices are returned, but after a quick scan you'll notice a your Raspberry Pi connected to the network. From here you can discover the IP address of your Pi.

Troubleshooting Pi Camera issue

If your Pi reboots as soon as you run the commands, your power supply is insufficient for running your Pi plus the camera module (and whatever other peripherals you have attached).

Pi Camera not detected - double check the connection of the ribbon cable to the camera and CSI connector, this can become loose over a period of time, especially if you travel with the Pi a lot. Using a fingernail, flip up the connector on the PCB, then reconnect it with gentle pressure.
If something else happens, read the error message displayed and try any recommendations suggested by the error messages -

- Error : raspistill/raspivid command not found. This probably means your update/upgrade commands failed in some way. Try the commands again, and ensure you are connected to the internet.
- Error : ENOMEM. The Camera Module is not starting up. Check all connections again.
- Error : ENOSPC. The Camera Module is probably running out of GPU memory. Check config.txt in the /boot/ folder. The gpu_mem option should be at least 128. Alternatively, use the Memory Split option in the Advanced section of raspi-config to set this.

After a few months, you may observe the picture captured with a camera is either blank or black. This issue occurs due to the old versions of packages installed. While using the Raspberry Pi, make sure all the packages installed on the Raspberry Pi are up-to-date. To resolve this issue, run commands to upgrade the packages on the Raspberry Pi OS using -

pi@raspberrypi:~ $ sudo apt update && sudo apt full-upgrade -y

Using dmesg command for debugging

dmesg is a display message command, that display kernel-related messages on linux operating systems. The output contains messages produced by the device drivers. The Linux kernel is the core of the operating system that controls access to the system resources, such as central processing unit, Input/Output devices, physical memory, and file systems. The kernel writes several messages to the kernel ring buffer during the boot process and when the system is running.

dmesg is used to examine or control the kernel ring buffer. It is really useful for examining kernel boot messages and debugging hardware related issues. Since Pi is a non-root user you will have to use sudo to run the dmesg command.

pi@raspberrypi:~ $ sudo dmesg

To monitor real-time logs --follow option is used with dmesg, and it displays the recent messages at the bottom of the terminal

pi@raspberrypi:~ $ sudo dmesg --follow

If you find the dmesg output to be too large you can use the tail option with the pipe operator, this is something we covered in Chapter V.

pi@raspberrypi:~ $ sudo dmesg | tail -10

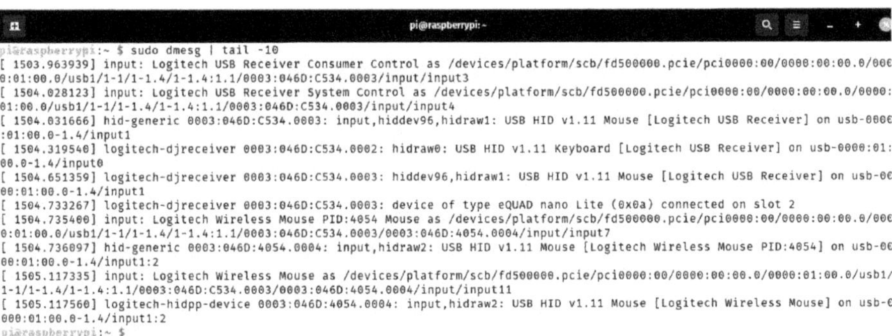

In case, you are debugging a specific issue with respect to a USB device you just connected to the Pi, you can use grep with the -i option to perform

- Orange - Percentage of RAM being used for cache memory.

Task statistics - the right-hand side part of the screen shows the task statistics

- The first entity '34' represents the number of current tasks/processes in the system.
- These 34 processes are handled by '31' number of threads (thr).
- Among 31 tasks, only a single task is in the state of running.
- Load Average – Since this is a quad-core system, the maximum amount of load is 4.0. The values mentioned are moving averages over different periods of time, that is for a minute, the last 5 minutes and last 15 minutes.
- Uptime – 49 minutes and 41 seconds, is the amount of time since the last system reboot.

Process Information - The bottom part of the htop command shows a vast amount of information for each process in the system. Each process comprises of the following information-

- PID (Process ID) – Unique number designated to the process.
- USER – The owner of the process.
- PRI (Priority) – The kernel's priority for the process.
- NI (Nice Value) – The process priority as viewed by the USER. (Higher nice value – Lower priority).
- VIRT (Virtual Memory) – The amount of virtual memory the process is consuming.
- RES (Resident Memory) – The proportion of RAM the process is using.
- SHR (Shared Memory) – The amount of shared memory the task is occupying.
- S (Status) – The current state of the process, S – Sleeping, R – Running, etc.
- CPU% – The percentage of CPU used by the process.
- MEM% – The percentage of Memory consumed by the process.
- TIME+ – The period of time since the process initiated.

- Command – The complete command for the process with program name and arguments

htop also provides interactive options at the bottom with option like help, setup to customize the look and feel of the htop screen. He are some must try options -

- Filter through the processes (F4) - instead of searching for keywords among all the process listed using Search for a Process (F3) option, it is easier to only display those processes matching the keyword. Press the F4 key, and enter the word that you want to filter the processes with. Try filtering the WiFi network related process, by searching for 'wpa'.

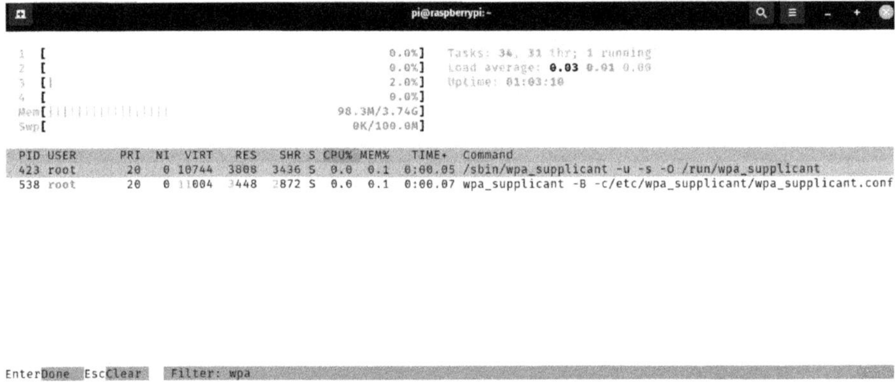

- Sort By(F6) - Pressing the 'F6' key, takes us to the sorting screen. By default, the processes are sorted on the basis of CPU usage %. Using the arrow keys, we can select other parameters for sorting.
- Kill a process(F9) - Selecting a process, and pressing the F9 key, leads to killing the process. Linux handles the killing of tasks automatically when the command or process exits. Unless you need to, there won't be any need to manually kill tasks. This normally comes handy when an application is hung.

Task Manager, which can be opened from the Accessories section of the Application menu, also provides similar functionality but in a graphical interface, by making using of mouse. And is similar to Microsoft Windows Task Manager, as discussed in chapter IV.

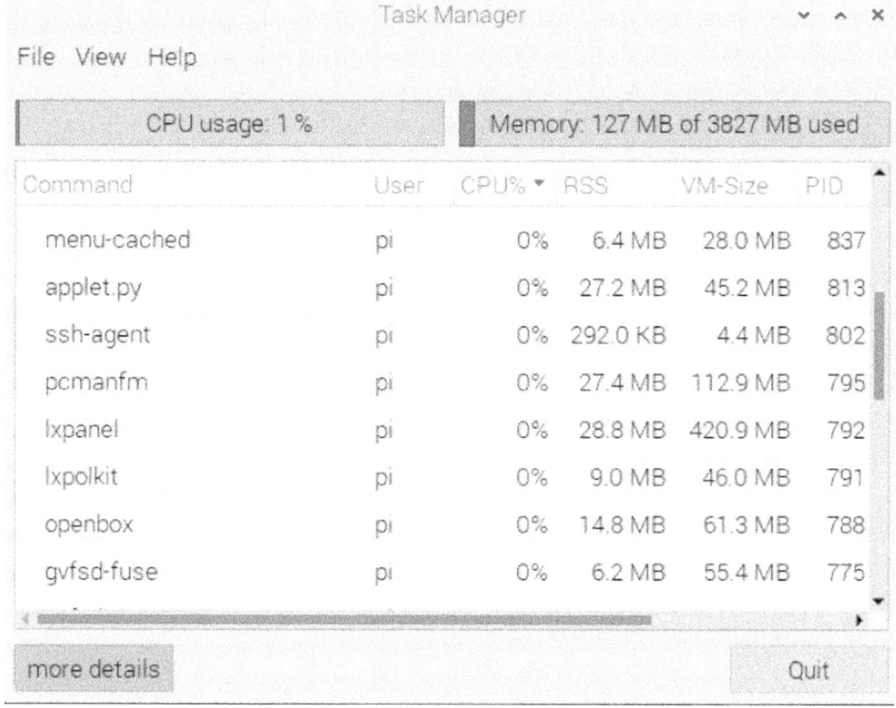

Glossary

1-Wire

1-Wire protocol is a single-wire interface for low-speed data communication in microcontrollers and computers. The protocol operates over a single data line without a clock signal. It's a master-slave serial communication protocol where the half-duplex bidirectional data communication with multiple slaves is solely managed and controlled by a single master.

Accelerometer

Accelerometers are devices that measure acceleration, which is the rate of change of the velocity of an object. They measure in meters per second squared (m/s2) or in G-forces (g).

AT&T

AT&T Inc. is an American multinational telecommunications holding company headquartered in Dallas, Texas. It is the world's largest telecommunications company by revenue and the third largest provider of mobile telephone services in the United States of America.

DRM-free

DRM-free refers to media without digital rights management (DRM). DRM-free technology permits software to bypass access control technologies used in media protected by copyright laws.

eMMC

An embedded MultiMediaCard (eMMC) is a small storage device/chip. eMMC acts as the primary storage for portable devices like cell phones or tablets, and also available on the Pi Compute modules, to store the operating system and can be further augmented using an microSD card.

fps

Frame rate (expressed in frames per second or FPS) is the frequency (rate) at which consecutive images (frames) are captured or displayed.

Gigabit Ethernet

Gigabit Ethernet is a transmission technology based on the Ethernet frame format and protocol used in local area networks (LANs), provides a data rate of 1 billion bits per second, or 1 gigabit (Gb).

GPIO

General Purpose Input Output. The Raspberry Pi has two rows of GPIO pins, which are connections between the Raspberry Pi, and the real world. Output pins are like switches that the Raspberry Pi can turn on or off (like turning on/off a LED light). But it can also send a signal to another device.

GPU

Graphics Processing Unit is a specialized electronic circuit designed to manipulate and alter memory to accelerate the creation of images in a frame buffer intended for output to a display device.

GNU

GNU is an operating system that is free software - that is, it respects users' freedom. The GNU operating system consists of GNU packages (programs specifically released by the GNU Project) as well as free software released by third parties. The development of GNU made it possible to use a computer without software that would trample your freedom.

Gyroscope

Gyroscopes are small, inexpensive sensors that measure angular velocity. The units of angular velocity are measured in degrees per second (°/s) or revolutions per second (RPS). Angular velocity is simply a measurement of speed of rotation.

I2C

The Inter-Integrated Circuit (I2C) Protocol is a protocol intended to allow multiple "peripheral" digital integrated circuits ("chips") to communicate with one or more "controller" chips. I2C requires a mere two wires (data and clock), like asynchronous serial, but those two wires can support up to 1008 peripheral devices.

initrd

The initial RAM disk (initrd) is an initial root file system that is mounted prior to when the real root file system is available. The initrd is bound to the kernel and loaded as part of the kernel boot procedure. The kernel then mounts this initrd as part of the two-stage boot process to load the modules to make the real file systems available and get at the real root file system.

Kernel
The Linux® kernel is the main component of a Linux operating system (OS) and is the core interface between a computer's hardware and its processes. It communicates between the two, managing resources as efficiently as possible.

Lego
Lego, consists of variously colored interlocking plastic bricks accompanying an array of gears, figurines called minifigures, and various other parts. Lego pieces can be assembled and connected in many ways to construct objects, including vehicles, buildings, and working robots. Anything constructed can be taken apart again, and the pieces reused to make new things.

LXDE
LXDE (abbreviation for Lightweight X11 Desktop Environment) is a free desktop environment with comparatively low resource requirements. This makes it especially suitable for use on older or resource-constrained personal computers such as netbooks or system on a chip computers, like the Raspberry Pi.

Magnetometer
Magnetometer also known as a magnetic sensor, is a sensor for measuring magnetic induction (magnetic field intensity).The magnetometer sensor measures the magnetic field for all three physical axes (x, y, z) in μT (micro Tesla).

NES
The Nintendo Entertainment System (NES) is an 8-bit third-generation home video game console produced by Nintendo. It included games like Super Mario, Zelda, Contra and more.

PCIe interface
Peripheral Component Interconnect Express is an interface standard for

connecting high-speed components. Every desktop PC motherboard has a number of PCIe slots you can use to add GPUs (also called graphics cards), Wi-Fi cards or SSD (solid-state drive for storage) and other add-on cards.

ROMs
In the context of gaming, ROM is a digital copy of a video game. ROMs provide the possibility of playing older games on newer computers or mobile phones. There are public domain ROMs available for NES, Arcade and Gameboy.

Serial(Rx,Tx)
A simple serial protocol consists of just two wires, one for sending data and another for receiving. As such, serial devices should have two serial pins, the receiver, RX, and the transmitter, TX.

SPI - Serial Peripheral Interface (SPI) is a synchronous interface which allows several SPI microcontrollers to be interconnected. In SPI, separate wires are required for data and clock line. Also the clock is not included in the data stream and must be furnished as a separate signal. The SPI may be configured either as master or as a slave.

Threads - Threads are the virtual components or codes, which divides the physical core of a CPU into virtual multiple cores. A single CPU core can have upto 2 threads per core.For example, if a CPU is dual core (2 cores) it will have 4 threads. And if a CPU is Octal core (8 core) it will have 16 threads and vice-versa.

References

Raspberry Pi Websites

- https://www.raspberrypi.org/
- https://codeclubworld.org/
- https://coderdojo.com/
- https://www.raspberrypi.org/jam/

Magazine - https://magpi.raspberrypi.com/
Free books - https://www.raspberrypi.com/books-magazines/
Datasheets - https://datasheets.raspberrypi.com/

Famous Projects using the Pi

- https://kodi.tv/
- https://yatse.tv/
- https://retropie.org.uk/
- https://github.com/motioneye-project
- https://github.com/pi-hole/pi-hole
- https://developer.amazon.com/en-US/docs/alexa/alexa-smart-screen-sdk/raspberry-pi.html
- https://learn.pimoroni.com/article/getting-started-with-enviro-plus
- https://www.home-assistant.io/
- https://octoprint.org/

Downloading Raspberry Pi OS

- **For Pi 4** - https://www.raspberrypi.com/software/
- **For PC and Mac** -https://www.raspberrypi.com/software/raspberry-pi-desktop/
- **Etcher to flash Raspberry Pi OS on SD card** - https://www.balena.io/etcher/

Software Installed on Pi

- Minecraft - https://www.minecraft.net/en-us/edition/pi
- Libreoffice - https://www.libreoffice.org/
- Scratch - https://www.scratchfoundation.org/
- Thonny Python IDE -https://thonny.org/
- Sense HAT Emulator - https://sense-emu.readthedocs.io/
- Sonic Pi - https://sonic-pi.net/
- GIMP - https://www.gimp.org/
- Claws Mail - https://www.claws-mail.org/
- Filezilla - https://filezilla-project.org/
- VNC viewer - https://www.realvnc.com/en/connect/download/viewer/

Using Pi camera

- https://www.raspberrypi.com/documentation/accessories/camera.html
- **FFmpeg** - https://www.ffmpeg.org/about.html
- **ImageMagick** - https://imagemagick.org/script/convert.php

Shell Scripting

- https://en.wikipedia.org/wiki/Shell_script
- https://wiki.debian.org/systemd
- https://en.wikipedia.org/wiki/Cron

www.ingramcontent.com/pod-product-compliance
Ingram Content Group UK Ltd.
Pitfield, Milton Keynes, MK11 3LW, UK
UKHW021915190726
13853UKWH00002B/677

9 798888 338476